GOD-IMAGES

GOD-IMAGES
IN THE
HEALING PROCESS

M. KATHRYN ARMISTEAD

FORTRESS PRESS   MINNEAPOLIS

GOD-IMAGES
In the Healing Process

This publication is designed to provide accurate and authoritative information in regard to the subject matter covered. It is sold with the understanding that the publisher is not engaged in rendering legal, accounting, or other professional services. If legal advice or other expert assistance is required, the services of a competent professional person should be sought. *From a Declaration of Principles jointly adopted by the Committee of the American Bar Association and a Committee of Publishers.*

Cover design: Evans McCormick Creative
Cover art: *Arboretum III* by Dan Mason
Text design: Lois Torvik

Library of Congress Cataloging-in-Publication Data

Armistead, M. Kathryn, 1952–
    God-images : in the healing process / M. Kathryn Armistead.
       p. cm.
    Includes bibliographical references.
    ISBN 0-8006-2586-2 (alk. paper)
      1. Counseling—Religious aspects—Christianity.   2. Image of God.
   3. Suffering—Religious aspects—Christianity. I. Title.
BR115.C69A76 1995
253.5—dc20
                                                95-23364
                                                    CIP

Manufactured in the U.S.A.   AF 1–2586

99   98   97   96   95   1   2   3   4   5   6   7   8   9   10

Contents

Acknowledgments

MANY PEOPLE HAVE played a part in helping me complete this book, and I want to express my appreciation to them. First, I want to thank my husband, Skip, who is an excellent counselor and minister. His steadfast support and pastoral experience helped me stay focused on and further delineate between the divine-human interface.

This book could not have been written without the intellectual prodding of my professors at Vanderbilt University during my time as a graduate student. I want to thank, in particular, Liston Mills, whose conviction it is that pastoral caregiving is essentially a theological task, and Volney Gay, who first introduced me to the importance of "Why me, now?"

I want to thank my former clients and others with whom I have stood on holy ground for what I have learned from them about the healing process. Their names and significant details of cases have been altered in the text to protect their identity.

Finally, I am indebted to my editors at Fortress Press: Tim Staveteig for his willingness to take a chance on a new author and Marshall Johnson for his encouragement.

Introduction

Religious Failure

JOHN WAS A twenty-five-year-old church member. He was happily married to his childhood sweetheart, Judith. Despite appearances, John lacked self-confidence, direction, and purpose for his life. He had tried various colleges and jobs. Judith had perseverance and charismatic leadership skills. She believed in her husband and lent him unswerving devotion.

John appeared to be a physically strong and active man, but he suffered from severe headaches. Judith was convinced that John smoked too much. They both thought that cigarettes along with his allergies brought on these "migraines." John, however, insisted that he enjoyed smoking and protested that he really was "all right."

Then one winter John really got sick. So sick that he allowed his name to be added to his church's prayer list. It seemed that he was constantly at the doctor's trying to find some relief from his headaches. Repeatedly Judith drove him to the emergency room at the local hospital for shots of painkiller. After several weeks the doctor refused to administer any more shots, accusing John of just wanting to get "high." Both John and Judith were devastated. Judith called their minister to enlist his support. The minister knew the physician personally and testified to the reality of John's suffering. After yet another trip to the emergency room, Judith decided they would try another doctor.

The new doctor was a specialist in a neighboring city. After many tests, the doctor reluctantly agreed to increase the dosage of John's prescription pain medication. But there was no relief. John lived with constant and terrible pain. John quit his job because he could no longer concentrate at work.

In desperation, John and Judith found yet another specialist who agreed to sever a nerve in John's forehead in an attempt to stop the incredible pain.

When John awoke after surgery, he was pain free. Both he and Judith were elated. Judith quickly called back home to relay the good news. The church community praised God for their answered prayers. Now John and Judith could get on with their lives!

Several weeks later, however, John's pain returned, but instead of being in the middle of his forehead, the pain shifted to his temples. Again, the doctor performed surgery, and again, John was pain free. Again the church celebrated. But in less than three months, John had to have surgery again. When the pain returned this time, John and Judith gave up. The limits of their insurance coverage had nearly been reached, and their financial resources were dwindling. John decided he would just have to live with the pain.

For three years, John and Judith lived a nightmare. John became addicted to narcotics. Their marriage suffered. All thoughts of having children were dismissed. Nevertheless, Judith finished college and took a full-time job to pay the bills. All through this time, however, they clung to their church. They had close friends who encircled them, prayed for them, and never gave up hope.

John and Judith depended on their church, but they actively served too. They gave their church their time and talents. People marveled that with such suffering in their lives they could give so much to others.

As time went by, John slumped into depression and became a shell of his former self. One could only guess that the scars on his face masked much deeper scars on his soul. After a while, people quit asking how he felt. They did not forget, but they did begin to give up hope. John asked that his name be dropped from the prayer list, embarrassed that it had been there so long.

Two more years passed. John was admitted to the hospital, and Judith was housed nearby. After consultation with both of them, the doctors took John off *all* his medication. That night, alone in his room, John began the withdrawal process. As he suffered, he had a vision of Jesus in which Jesus said, "Your sins are forgiven. You do not have to feel guilty anymore." John passed out. When he awoke, he was free of pain for the first time in years. The doctors examined him, and found that, indeed, his facial nerves had stopped throbbing.

It was a miracle! John and Judith knew that God had answered their prayers. The prayers of their faith community had encircled them. John was healed. There was even physical evidence to convince the skeptics. What a powerful testimony they could give! John insisted on leaving the hospital immediately, against the advice of the doctors.

For three months, John and Judith were cautious. They had been disappointed so many times, but God had never intervened like this before. For three months, life was normal. John got a job. Judith began to dream of building a house of their own and having children. Then the headaches returned. They asked, "What happened? Had they failed God in some way? What would they do now?"

That was five years ago. Today, John tries to live with his pain and depression. Judith goes to work every day. They go to church most Sundays. They still have their friends and family, but both are bitterly disappointed with their lives.

John and Judith are disappointed, but so is their church. John and Judith are good people. They are loving people. Surely Job did not suffer more. They do not deserve the life they are living.

If there is anything unusual about the story of John and Judith, it is *not* that John had a vision of Jesus, nor is it that their faith community encircled them with love and care. What is unusual and what invites admiration is that John and Judith are still faithful. Despite their bitterness, their disappointment, their feelings of rejection and abandonment and possibly anger toward God, John and Judith still turn toward God and their faith community.

Understanding Careseekers' Images of God

The purpose of this book is to help caregivers understand how careseekers image God. John saw an image of God. Some hear God's voice. Others feel surrounded by God's warmth. Many people experience God as a vividly real personal presence. This is *not* to say that these experiences of God are necessarily a comfort or that they might not provoke anxiety. It is to say, however, that someone who feels torn apart, shattered, empty, or utterly alone may turn to God in a powerful way. Many seek the companionship of God. Many may also seek God when they feel whole, but this book deals with people in crises.

I use this example of John and Judith because it is typical of actual caregiving. There are Johns and Judiths in many churches. Many people have similar experiences of God. Many know that God healed them. Many feel abandoned by their God. God often disappoints and angers people. This book will describe the importance of individuals' images of God to better equip caregivers for their task.

Experiences of God as a vividly real personal presence, while not commonplace, are common. People in the North and South, in urban and rural settings; senior citizens, adults, youth, and children—everyone has images of God. I find that the commonalities of God-images far outweigh the differences. I recall sitting with a group of ten teenagers at their regular Sunday night meeting. As we went around the circle, *each* youth shared a time when he or she *felt, saw, or heard* God's presence. And I recall another incident, which occurred in the home of one of our church members. As we sat in the living room, everyone was invited to share some faith experience as a part of our Bible study. Most of these people were elderly and had spent time in the hospital. Almost all of them told how God had healed them as they lay in their hospital beds. Many had seen a vision of Jesus or God's angels, and if they had not had such an experience personally, they all knew of someone who had.

Some people also experience an image of a devil. These experiences are often shared with great reluctance and fear. These experiences also merit study, but this issue is beyond the scope of this book.

As a religious caregiver, I do not have the luxury of *simply* saying that a vision of God or hearing God's voice is a psychotic episode. While it is significant that John experienced his vision while suffering withdrawal, it is not satisfactory to say that that is all it was. Why experience God? Why not Napoleon? Why did God say that John did not have to feel guilty anymore?

To dismiss John's vision as simply psychological is to ignore all that John and Judith have at stake. Their faith and the faith of their religious community are involved, including, perhaps, the faith of their pastor. One thing is certain: when John and Judith talked to their pastor, they expected him to understand their God. They even wished that the pastor would explain their God to them.

But how can we religious caregivers comprehend the careseeker's relationship with God? How can we understand what John's God said? Does it matter? Why did John's experience of God occur at that particular point in his life? What does it mean to John that God has not appeared since? If God is a focal point of his life, what does it mean to John that that point is now, at the very least, blurred? How does John's image of God correspond to the God of his faith community?

John is a good church member. He considers himself a practicing Christian. God's appearance in his hospital room did not really surprise him; in fact, he really wondered why God had not appeared sooner. All his life John had believed that God was a "ready source of help in time of trouble." John had been taught and had taught his own church school class to "expect a miracle." Now, when he needed God most, God helped him. No, God *saved* him from utter despair. In that hospital room, John felt really alone. He knew that he was in the valley of the shadow of death, and he feared evil. John longed for God's rod and staff and God's comfort.

How can we understand and help John understand his experience of God's presence? The question really is not why John was healed or why the pain returned. I, as a religious caregiver, believe that God's presence loves and comforts, perhaps admonishes and convicts, but God's presence never condemns or abandons anyone to the utter pain of solitude. (That is my faith statement. Each religious caregiver must come to his or her own affirmation of faith.)

For John, there was no question as to who healed him. John's faith tradition teaches that God intervenes in human history and offers salvation to God's children. John firmly believes that God was really present with him in a powerful way in that hospital room. For John, his experience of God is the "most real" thing that has ever happened to him. John is still so convinced that God healed him that he cannot even imagine God allowing the pain to return. John cannot even imagine that God would disappoint him.

But John was afraid to ponder the question that deeply concerned him: Why did God fail me? Until John wrestled with that question he lived with a punishing sense of guilt. It is easier for John to feel that he somehow deserved God's punishment than to risk wrestling with the possibility that his God failed him.

John has another faith question. Where is God's presence now? John still attends his church and is active in its programs. He loves his church family and they love him. But for John, God is not there. John believes that because his pain returned, God left his life. John goes to church to be sustained by the love God has for other people.

The purpose of telling John's story is not to pass judgment on John but to illustrate in a powerful way the entanglement of faith and psychological issues that can emerge from an experience of God's presence. When people hurt, they often turn to God. Many people experience the companionship of God. For many, this experience marks *the* important event in their personal faith story. Religious caregivers need a clearer way to think about these vividly real, personal encounters.

How does God come to be a particular part of an individual's life? Augustine said there is a place in our being that only God can fill. It seems to me that the dimensions of that place are specific to each person. My need of God is unique to me as an individual within this community, in this place, at this time. The God who fills my needy self makes God, in part, my God. My relationship with God may be more than that, to be sure, but my own images and my own experiences of God reflect my own uniqueness to some degree.

God interfaces with my faith community as well, but I relate to God out of my own human understanding, limited as that might be.

This book is about the human side of the divine-human interface. That is one reason psychological tools can be helpful. Yet the divine-human interface will always transcend psychology, as it transcends any human endeavor. The basic assumption of this book is that for effective ministry a caregiver must strive for clear understanding of a careseeker's experience of God.

Distressed people may turn toward caregivers as well as toward God. But when a distressed person intentionally seeks help from a member of a faith group, whether minister, chaplain, counselor, or friend, that caregiver may be sure that God is somehow an ingredient in providing relief, even if God is never specifically mentioned. So what is a caregiver to do? How can I, as a religious caregiver, be most effective? As a caregiver myself, I continually rediscover that the care a distressed person or family seeks from me is directly related to the kind of care he, she, or they expect from God. And, conversely, the kind of help expected from God is directly related to the kind of help expected from me. Hence, a relationship of greater depth and scope with a caregiver may provide careseekers a way of taking a "closer walk" with God. Likewise, a deeper faith in God may provide careseekers a way to enter into more intimate human relationships.

When John and Judith called their pastor, they expected that he would understand. They did not expect miracles, but they did expect explanations of God's mysterious behavior. But in the mind of their pastor, these expectations bore a striking similarity. The point is that they wanted to talk about God and their faith. They wanted to express their feelings; they wanted empathic listening, but more than that, they wanted deliverance.

Many are like John and Judith. They are part of the faith story of every religious community. Some are so afraid of being disappointed once again that they suffer in silence. Pastors, like others in the faith community, get tired, scared, angry, or humbled when faced with expectations of such proportions.

The Problem of God-Language

Historically, one of the problems in pastoral counseling has been what to do with God. There has been confusion about using "God-talk" in counseling; the fear is that the careseeker may think the caregiver is "preaching." The feeling that caregiving is an essential part of ministry, along with misgivings about what to do with God-language, may create what I call "double-mindedness" within the caregiver.

Psychologically, double-mindedness can be described as ambivalence. By ambivalence, I mean the opposite of certainty or of walking in one direction, whether walking toward, away from, or over and against. Before caregivers can empathically participate in a careseeker's God-language, they must at least be acquainted with the meaning of their own and be prepared to travel through the storms of careseekers' lives with some certainty.

Ambivalence about using God-language is very real today, particularly among those caregivers who received their clinical training or own therapy using models developed by psychologists such as Carl Rogers. Rogers is still an excellent resource. His emphasis on listening and acceptance remains a substantial contribution to the field of pastoral care and counseling, but as religious caregivers we must scrutinize Rogers' unspoken theological presuppositions. From a theological perspective his notions of unconditional positive regard and nonjudgmental understanding are beyond the scope of human achievement. Only God can give anything unconditionally: human beings by their very nature are judging and evaluating creatures.

It is no accident that pastoral care literature in the past ten to fifteen years has begun to reclaim and rediscover new appreciation for the theological heritage of our varied religious communities along with an increasing emphasis in pastoral care and counseling on the dynamics of responsible, ethical caregiving. The return to a theological grounding is applauded by such leaders in the field of pastoral care as Seward Hiltner, Wayne Oates, Thomas Oden, and others. Some, such as Donald Capps and Don Browning, seek to give a more secure theoretical grounding to pastoral care. But returning to a theological foundation also means returning to some theological problems, such as what to do with God and how to talk about God. Seeking a theological foundation, in some respects, has made the issue of who God is and who God ought to be more pressing for careseekers.

Many careseekers look for religious caregivers because faith in God is important to them. Careseekers often come with a presupposition that faith in God is also important to the person they wish to make their counselor. At the very least, they expect their caregiver to be fluent in God-language.

Some careseekers want comfort and relief not only from the caregiver but also from God. Being fluent in the God-language of various traditions enables me as a religious caregiver to deal openly and directly with religious presuppositions and expectations concerning the caring relationship. It also enables me to deal openly and directly with the images and symbols careseekers use in telling their stories. The issue for caregivers becomes what does language about God mean and how does it impact the caring relationship? That is, how does God-language embody feelings and convictions about the self and other? How do feelings about self and other impact personal images and language about God?

Premises

Being fluent in God-language is not enough. The caregiver must often look behind the careseeker's language to discern the unconscious weaving of images, feelings, and ideation. To do so requires a special kind of listening for certain kinds of things. The premise of this book is that a person's faith is the core of the self. This means that personality as an expression of self is a manifestation of a person's faith. By faith I mean those deeply felt values without which the self cannot be the self. When expressed in language, these values are realized as convictions or deeply held beliefs. And such convictions are always held with more than rational tenacity. The self, as I am describing it, is the dynamic embodiment and enactment of faith.

Historically, some cultures and persons have associated God-language with human essence and process. For example, Paul Tillich named God the "Ground of Being"—not just human being but all that is, was, and yet will be. While I am not a systematic theologian, I do understand the giving and receiving of care as an essentially theological endeavor. Seen in this light, giving care is a ministry best understood within the context of the church.

Caregiving and careseeking may or may not be couched in religious language. As caregivers set sail with careseekers through uncharted waters, they are free to discover and learn from the images of God they find, but other meaningful relationships will also emerge, expressed in rich language and imagery. With sails unfurled, they, and we, are free to catch the prevailing wind of the Spirit.

Methodological Questions

How does a caregiver understand a careseeker's faith, especially when it is understood as that which is most "holy" to the self? How does each person image that which is holy? What do those images say about the person as a unique human being? How do we journey with someone to the holy? Who stands behind those holy images? How do people break through those images to find greater depth and scope in their own interpersonal relating? What supplies do we need for such a journey? Once the holy is found, how do we get acquainted with whom we find? Once acquainted, how can the careseeker's other relationships be further nourished? This book offers caregivers psychological supplies for the journey.

Three authors whose work has helped me find answers to these questions are object relations theorist Ana-Maria Rizzuto, psychoanalyst Heinz Kohut, and psychologist Daniel Stern. For example, Rizzuto helped me answer the question, Why are an individual's God-images self-revealing? Rizzuto suggests in *Birth of the Living God* that God-images, or as she calls them "representations" of God, are important in maintaining a person's sense of mental balance. They evolve out of a person's earliest significant relationships with mother and father. Growing up shapes a person and his or her God-images. A child's world may create the child, but that world is also created and sustained, in part, by the child and his or her God-images.

Heinz Kohut, in *How Does Analysis Cure?* helped me answer the question, Why do individuals call upon God in the face of extreme anxiety? They need companionship. When someone feels shattered, torn apart, wounded "to the quick," only another person will do. For some, only God will do. For some, only God can soothe and repair the tragic needs of the self.

Kohut observed that when a person feels shattered or coming apart—unglued, shredded, or engulfed by the "black hole" within—that person has a means through self-experience to put the self back together again, to put the self "back on track," or even "lick his or her wounds." The person creates a new experience by interacting with an image of interpersonal experience to effect repairs of the self. This is not simply recalling a benevolent memory or an escape into pleasant childhood fantasy; it is a healthy response of a maturing person whose self as he or she knows it is threatened. The term that Kohut uses to designate this personal representation of interpersonal experience that is called upon in the face of anxiety is "selfobject."

Selfobjects originate in the lifelong human need for other people to confirm and affirm a personal self. By "self," I mean that cohesive and enduring sense of being an independent center of initiative and perception. A person has many kinds of interpersonal relationships that make up different selfobjects. What we are interested in here is the interpersonal relationship between the self and God as it is imaged by the person.

A God-image is self-revealing. Careseekers may call upon the companionship of a personal God in the face of extreme anxiety. But what does it mean for God to be experienced as an immanently real, personal presence here and now? Stern's work is helpful in answering this question.

Rizzuto shows us how we can psychologically understand a personal image of God. Kohut gives us a way to understand companionship with God. Stern enables us to understand that immanently real interpersonal experience with careseekers.

In the following chapters I will explore the significance of images of God in the lives of four careseekers, using examples and some extended case studies. Then, in the final chapter, I shall consider some implications and offer suggestions for further inquiry.

— 1 —

Standing on Holy Ground

WHAT IS THE most real thing that has ever happened to you? Many religious persons would immediately say, "An encounter with God."

We all have an image of God. Whether one is a believer or an atheist, whether one sings in a church choir or plays golf on Sunday mornings, whether one is five or ninety-five, we all have some image of God. This fact alone makes an individual's image of God significant. In our culture, in our everyday world, various idiosyncratic gods move, intermingle, and clash. Various religious groups vie for the individual's loyalty to God, perhaps seeking to mold and make the individual's image of God into one acceptable and accessible to the larger group.

The patriarch Jacob found holy ground in a dream along the side of the road at Bethel (Gen. 28:13–15). Now recall John, the man with incurable head pain. John found holy ground in a hospital room.

After years of pain and consequent addiction to narcotics, John entered a hospital. As he began the withdrawal process, John felt terribly alone and afraid. As he suffered, he had a vision of Jesus. Jesus appeared as a tall man with a flowing beard and white robe. But what really caught John's attention was not what Jesus looked like but what he said: "Your sins are forgiven. You do not have to feel guilty anymore."

John felt a tremendous sense of relief. Then he passed out and slept, pain free. John later said that when he felt the real, personal presence of God in that hospital room, he was too weak to resist. When Judith, John's wife, arrived the following morning, she could hardly believe it. It was a miracle! God answered their prayers. Judith immediately relayed the news back home.

For John there was no longer a reason to stay in the hospital. When the doctors arrived later to examine him, John told them he was going home. The doctors advised against leaving. After all, John's body had undergone a

1

tremendous shock. But John was resolute. That same day, John and Judith took a flight home. Friends and well-wishers met them, eager to share the joy.

John and Judith were cautious at first; they had been disappointed so many times. But this time was different: God had intervened in a new way. Life slowly drifted back to normal. John got a job; Judith began to hope for building their home and having children at last. But then John's headaches returned.

At first John did not tell anyone, not even his wife. Surely it was a mistake. "Surely," he thought, "I must have the flu." But the pain was real, and it slowly took over his life again. John despaired, but Judith was not about to give up now. She called their pastor. "Come!" she said, "Something terrible has happened."

In this chapter we will look at how a caregiver moves with a person so that together they may stand on holy ground. John encountered God. This encounter occurred while John was undergoing drug withdrawal. According to John, God forgave his guilt and then took the pain away. John made an association between his physical pain and his guilt. For John, removal of pain meant absence of guilt. The return of pain also meant return of guilt.

Why had John immediately left the hospital after his experience with God? Was he fleeing further insight? Was he afraid of what might happen if he stayed? Did he believe he needed nothing else from God? Or did he believe that that was all God could do for him? How are we to understand John's continued faith in a seemingly capricious God? How could John put his hope in God again? Helping John explore his holy ground helped John deal with questions. But first a caregiver has to stand on holy ground *with* the careseeker. John found holy ground, but he needed the empathic presence of another to understand what he found.

Most relationships between caregivers and careseekers do not begin on holy ground. Counseling usually begins with a crisis. Judith made a call to the pastor, not because she and John were undergoing a faith crisis, but because she needed someone to drive John to the local hospital for a shot of painkiller. The purpose of this chapter is to guide caregivers toward being an empathic presence, thereby extending the depth and scope of the careseeker's holy ground. This empathic presence enables careseekers more fully to understand their own relationship with God.

I am concerned with individual caregiving. While other modalities are important, they are also more interpersonally complicated. In this book I focus on individual counseling in an attempt to keep the variables as simple as possible. Even with two people physically present in a room, there are the caregiver as she understands herself and the careseeker, as well as the careseeker as understood by him- or herself and the caregiver.

Why Me, Now?

In order to be present with a careseeker on holy ground, the caregiver must begin with the question, Why me, now? As John sat in the pastor's study, the pastor thought about his personal feelings toward John. The pastor knew it would be difficult to be objective. But why was John refusing to see anyone else for counseling? The pastor asked John to reflect on that question. John said doctors continued to disappoint him, and he was tired of strangers who did not really know him or care about him. "Further, I feel funny talking to them about God. You, on the other hand, are a long-standing, trusted friend. I think you'll understand."

Why begin with "Why me, now?" Because this question focuses the caregiver on the relationship between the caregiver and careseeker from the beginning. This simple question also guides the caregiver toward other related questions. Why did this careseeker seek me, a particular kind of caregiver, at this time in this way? What is so special about this situation that this certain person would seek me out in particular?

John came to a pastor who was also his understanding, trusted friend, but the pastor unearthed other reasons. John was angry at his doctors. In John's eyes they failed him and belittled his religion. Further, the pastor would not charge any money for his counseling. This last consideration was important, because John's financial resources were nil. But as the counseling process deepened, the pastor also found out that John chose him because of what being a "trusted friend" meant. It meant knowing when to "back off." By choosing the pastor, John was choosing someone who, John thought, would let him control the degree of interpersonal intimacy. Thus part of the counseling process inevitably involved redefining how the pastor was and was not a trusted friend. In so doing, John also experienced a new kind of trust.

This question of "Why me, now?" is important particularly for local church pastors who see counseling as part of their total ministry. These pastors generally do not charge a fee for counseling. This can be both a blessing and curse for prospective careseekers. It is a blessing because many folks who need counseling the most just do not have the money. But it is a curse, because people tend to believe the more a service is worth (and the more they themselves are worth), the more it costs. This issue is hotly debated among clergy, pastoral counselors, and other caregivers. Money is generally part of the "Why me, now?" question and must be considered.

Framing the Counseling Relationship

As the caregiver begins to find answers to the "Why me, now?" question, he or she also begins to frame the counseling relationship, defining the rules or boundaries under which the counseling will proceed. This process is more difficult for local church pastors than for other caregivers. Framing implies a degree of control that local church pastors do not have. For example, the pastor's home phone number is often common knowledge. Careseekers generally have more access to the private life of the pastor. Careseekers may see the pastor at informal social events like church suppers. In some cases, a careseeker may be an important contributor to the pastor's salary. While these issues may not seem important at the onset, they may become significant ingredients in the counseling relationship. Despite the pastor's own fear of failure, he could also see that John's life was getting more unmanageable. John thought about suicide "all the time." Judith threatened to move out. John and the pastor decided they would begin meeting one hour a week. The pastor suggested that they keep a regular meeting schedule. If John wanted to meet more often, he could call the pastor for an appointment. The pastor also insisted that John see his physician and strictly abide by the prescribed dosage of pain medication. Further, the pastor advised Judith to watch John closely and find a caregiver to address her own needs.

Using his authority as a caregiver, the pastor entered into an agreement with John to shore up the boundaries of counseling. In so doing the pastor began to create a sanctuary of time and place in which John could feel secure enough to trust.

Getting Started

So John, an eager careseeker, began seeing a cautious pastor. During the first session, the pastor tried to get a clear picture of how John came to be in his study. What triggered John's decision to seek out counseling with him? What did "being in counseling" mean to John? To John being in counseling was an admonition of failure. He felt deeply embarrassed and ashamed of not being able to handle his own problems. What were his problems? There was the constant pain, but John also felt depressed and depleted. He was worn out. At times he felt that he might "go up in smoke."

The pastor spoke to John in an encouraging voice, urging John to go at his own pace. The pastor told him how important it was to speak freely, trying not to censor thoughts and avoid feelings. During these first sessions, the pastor was as observant as possible, noting John's tone of voice, body posture, breathing patterns, as well as hearing the thoughts and feelings that John expressed. How did John open the sessions? How did he leave? The pastor noted as much as possible in order to find patterns in their interrelating. What provoked anxiety? What diminished it? The pastor also monitored his own thoughts, feelings, and behavior. What drew him closer to John? What pushed him away? What raised or diminished his own anxieties?

As the first few sessions unfolded it became clear that John was a dependent person. He had a hard time leaving the pastor's study. Each week he saved something significant to tell the pastor just as it was time to go. The pastor thought that John clung to these sessions as a child hangs onto a mother's skirt. In fact, the pastor noted to himself that John acted like a little boy much of the time. John's voice was soft and high pitched. He often sat with his head down, not looking the pastor in the eyes. For the first three months constantly and occasionally after that, John confessed many of what he called "wicked" and "sinful" thoughts for which he was sure God would punish him. He often asked permission to sit in the chair he wanted and would pull it close to the pastor's. When the pastor spoke, John cowered. The first time he did this, it was so striking the pastor automatically turned around to see if there was someone else standing behind him.

Recalling Memories

After three months during which John acted like a little boy and seemed to cast the pastor in the role of a punishing parent, the pastor mentioned that he was surprised that John seemed to respond as a little child. The pastor wondered aloud if John recognized this and what it might mean. John was taken aback. Had he failed the pastor? He said he had assumed that was what the pastor wanted. Had he done something wrong?

As a result, John recounted this vivid memory. When John was about five years old, his mother sent him out of the house because she had to do "something" to his baby brother. She had to nurse him, and apparently it would be "wrong" and "dirty" if John saw her. But John peeked in the bedroom window and saw anyway. A little later, John's three-year-old brother came up to him and asked him for a drink. John sent him into the garage where he said there was a jar full of water. John said that he knew full well what was in that jar, and it was not water but kerosene. As John spoke, tears streamed down his face and sobs interrupted him. He said he wanted his brother to drink the kerosene, and he did.

John said he wanted his brother to die, and he would have if their father had not found him lying on the garage floor. John's father and mother hurriedly gathered the children into the car and rushed to the hospital. In the excitement, however, John was left behind, alone. Later, John's father asked John if he knew what had happened. Didn't he know that kerosene could poison his brother? John lied and said he did not know what was in the jar. John said he felt terribly afraid he would be punished anyway, but he never was. His lie was never found out. John was glad his brother did not die, but he was glad his brother suffered.

While telling this story, John kept looking at the pastor, scanning his face. The pastor was shocked. John appeared so meek and mild. But how much of this had actually happened? Was this a screen memory (a condensation of many memories that, when portrayed as a single event, signifies what it means for a person to be a self here and now)? The memory did describe, among other things, a traumatic failure of both parents: the mother's rejection and preference for another sibling and her refusal to share a secret sexual part of herself with him; the father's inability and perhaps impotence at not being able to uncover John's lie; and both parents' abandonment of him at a critical time. From that day forth, John said, neither parent seemed as big.

John and the pastor returned several times to this memory during their time together. It was John's earliest memory and the first childhood story recounted to the pastor, but the pastor wondered what its meaning was for the counseling relationship, the "us" in the here and now.

The Nature of Memory

When a careseeker relates a memory, how is the caregiver to understand it? Whether memory is the essence of mental processes or not is debatable, but all agree that memory is an important function of the mind. A memory is a recollection of representations. Representations are dynamic unconscious weavings of images, feelings, and ideations, which converge as a result of a developmental process of elaboration. Memory is a reconstructive process based *on* the past but not *of* the past. That is, memory is a function of the present. Transforming memories is what the mind does. What one remembers when with a caregiver, for example, is largely a matter of inference based on the current relationship between the caregiver and careseeker. And the caregiver's reactions to the self of the careseeker, both real and imagined, are instrumental in determining memories. And a change in the reported memory within the context of care is to a degree a function of the caring relationship itself.

Experiences are fixed in memory not as a record of particular events but as part of a scheme or patterning of similar experiences. To remember an event or person entails integrating and assimilating the total relationship within that event with that person. This is to say, any memory called to mind is a function of its interpersonal context.

Hence the pastor's question was well founded. What was "triggered" in the caring relationship that such a memory was evoked? When the pastor remarked that John acted like a little boy, John responded with a memory, not just any memory, but a key memory that later served to unlock many doors. John interpreted the pastor's remark as a failure by the pastor to understand him. John responded with an image of his mother with whom he wanted intimate closeness. John's memory also contained an image of a father who failed to uncover John's secret. John's response to his caregiver also expressed how he felt toward the pastor and what he wanted and feared the pastor would uncover.

But what exactly did the pastor fail to understand? Perhaps John felt rebuked because the pastor thought of him as a little boy. The pastor asked John to reflect on how it felt to be a little boy with him. From the pastor's tone of voice, John understood that the pastor was rejecting his behavior as childish. In John's mind, the pastor had rebuked him and "put him out" as his mother "put him out" when he was five. The tone of voice reminded John of his mother.

Seeing the World from the Careseeker's Point of View

A goal in caregiving is to enter into the careseeker's private world. To do this, one focuses on personal expressions of meaning. For example, what were John's thoughts and feelings associated with being a little boy just then with the pastor? Expressions of meaning include not only the cognitive reflections and fantasies, but also the associated feelings. In response to the pastor's invitation to "Tell me more," John burst forth with angry tears. "How dare you act like you know everything! You just can't imagine how hard it is for me to sit here week after week baring my soul to you, and afterwards you just get up and go home." "You feel close to me?" "Yes, and it angers me that you don't need me like I need you." "Part of you wishes that you could go home with me? Your anger seems to be a way you use to hide your fears about feeling close to me." "Yes." Then John sobbed.

How did the pastor go from John's remark about the pastor getting up and going home to "You feel close to me"? The pastor suddenly felt a longing on John's part. The pastor sensed that underneath the anger was something else, and from hours of patiently listening to John, he knew that John often used his anger to reach out. So the pastor reflected back what he sensed.

Insight: A Goal of Counseling

A goal of counseling is to move the careseeker toward insight, which means greater self-understanding of thoughts, feelings, and actions, but it also means congruence between thoughts, feelings, and actions. This means that when the careseeker verbally describes a loss, for example, he or she feels appropriate sadness, and acts sad; for example, tears may well up. There is also a related phenomenon. There are times when a careseeker may look, sound, and say he or she is feeling an emotion, but the caregiver feels no corresponding inner emotional resonance. This may mean a number of things, but in all events it should be noted by the caregiver. This may indicate an unconscious obstacle within the careseeker or the caregiver.

The Role of Empathy

The tool by which a caregiver gains entry into the inner world of a careseeker is empathy. Through empathy the caregiver understands what it means for the careseeker to be a self. Through empathy the careseeker observes and monitors both self and other. By empathy I mean vicarious introspection, a notion that puts us clearly within the scope of self psychology.

Heinz Kohut

Self psychology, a continuing evolution of psychoanalytic psychology founded by Sigmund Freud, was fundamentally shaped and articulated by Heinz Kohut. One of Kohut's major contributions to psychoanalytic thought is that there are not one but two developmental lines. One line leads to mature love of other people and other areas of human interest outside the individual. Other people and areas of human interest outside the self are objects toward which the self maneuvers. Object love is emotional investment devoid of self-interest, as Freud suggested. Hence for Freud the culmination of mature personhood is to love another selflessly and to work loyally.

But there is another line of development that leads to mature narcissism. The first line of development leads to mature relationships with other people and interests in areas of human endeavor outside the individual. The second line of development leads to a mature relationship with one's self. Kohut says quite clearly that narcissism does not blossom into object love. Narcissism is an investment of the self toward the self. Kohut points out that just as there are infantile, mature, and pathological ways a person can love objects, there are infantile, mature, and pathological ways a person can love him- or herself. Hence maturity is self-fulfillment in loving others and pride in accomplishing while at the same time realizing others will sometimes disappoint us and our accomplishments will be limited.

Empathy Defined

Empathy is a value-neutral tool of observation. It is a means by which the caregiver maintains what Kohut calls an "experience-near" perspective and from which the caregiver crafts interpretations. It is immersion into the careseeker's experience, which focuses the caregiver's attention upon what it is like to be the subject rather than the target, the object, of the careseeker's wishes and demands. Empathy is not what the caregiver guesses, intuits, or magically perceives going on in the mind of the careseeker. It is not being flooded by or taking over the feelings of another. It is rather the elegant tool of observation.

Because empathy is a tool, it can lead to correct or incorrect results. It can operate either rapidly and outside awareness or slowly and deliberately with focused conscious attention. Because empathy is a tool, it can be more or less skillfully employed. Empathy is a learned process that must be effectively used by a therapist if there is to be any good in the counseling relationship at all. Kohut even hints that the more empathic a caregiver is, the more curative therapy will be, because the more empathic one is, the better one is able to experience the inner life of another while simultaneously retaining the stance of an objective observer.

The Place of Cognitive Processes in Empathy

Empathy, whether it operates inside or outside of awareness, involves the mediation of cognitive processes. Daniel Stern, who offers a constructive dialogue between psychoanalytic theory and developmental psychology, suggests that empathy consists of at least four distinct and probably sequential processes: (1) resonance with the feeling states of another person, (2) abstraction of empathic knowledge from the interpersonal experience of emotional resonance, (3) integration of that abstracted knowledge with an empathic response, and (4) a transient role identification. Cognitive process is essential to empathy. That is why an appropriate empathic response by the caregiver yields increased understanding of the careseeker.

Empathy: The Key to Feeling Understood

Empathic response enables the careseeker to feel that he or she is understood by the caregiver, because it is expressed to the careseeker as a description of the careseeker's inner state. Empathic explanation demonstrates to the careseeker that the caregiver understands and to some extent experiences what the careseeker is experiencing, whether that be joy, emptiness, or enhanced self-esteem. Hence the pastor understood his own feelings of longing as an empathic response to John's.

Once the careseeker feels understood—and this may take many hours in counseling—the caregiver can offer an interpretation or explanation. The pastor interpreted to John that anger was a way John dealt with his fears of intimacy.

Juanita came to a caregiver because she said she felt frustrated in her "dead-end" job. The caregiver listened to Juanita's description of her empty feelings and dull existence. During this initial phase of the counseling relationship all Juanita seemed to want from the caregiver was a silent presence. When verbal exchanges occurred they often took the form of Juanita saying, "Uh," and the caregiver saying in response, "Ahuh." Juanita would then reply, "Ahuh." The caregiver would again say, "Ahuh." This sequence would occur three or four times, and then Juanita would continue her monologue. The caregiver noted to herself when these exchanges occurred. She observed that Juanita sought confirmation when she felt puzzled by her own feelings, and specifically when she felt anxiety related to sexuality. After many hours of counseling, Juanita explained that those exchanges were enough to let her know that the caregiver was a nonthreatening presence and that she understood Juanita's feelings.

The "uh/ahuh" exchanges, although very simple utterances—they were not really words—were as much of a description of Juanita's inner state as she could initially stand. Only much later was the caregiver invited to say much more.

The Place of Interpretation

After a careseeker feels understood, the caregiver may offer an explanation or interpretation. Interpretation is crucial to the counseling process, because it enables an empathic bonding between the careseeker and caregiver. This bond begins to guide the careseeker toward more mature relationships. That is, when the caregiver offers his or her own insights about the careseeker's motivations or reconstructions of the careseeker's history of relating, the caregiver retains an objective view. This enables the careseeker to experience a more objective view of himself or herself.

The Limits of Empathy

According to Kohut, empathy is limited to what is cognitively available to the person. Empathy is limited to what can be verbalized by a person about the self. This means that one cannot empathize with an infant or any other person who does not have a sense of self that he or she can verbally apprehend. This is a debatable point that needs further clarification, for there are other ways, such as music, to enter into another's inner world, but such a discussion is beyond the scope of this chapter. That Juanita could only tolerate "Ahuh" from her caregiver suggests that she had a very fragile sense of self, and her own empathy toward herself was very limited. Juanita was not resisting the caregiver but was entering into an interpersonal relationship as best she could. The scope and depth of the counseling relationship was very limited, because that was all the self Juanita had to offer. Yet Juanita had a rich inner world, and eventually through many hours of empathic listening, she let her caregiver share part of it. Through empathy, the caregiver supplied enough understanding to build an interpersonal bridge between herself and Juanita.

Empathic Failure

Through empathy, the relationship of John with his pastor proceeded in the direction of greater depth and scope. John began to feel that he was being understood. This is not to say, however, that the pastor always understood. There were inevitably times when the pastor failed, for example, when the pastor told John that he was acting like a child. The pastor meant "childlike," but John heard "childish." This was an empathic failure. But John responded. He felt rejected. He felt angry, hurt, and ashamed, but John was sufficiently emotionally bonded to the pastor that he could feel misunderstood and still maintain trust in the pastor. Technically speaking, they had a strong therapeutic alliance.

John responded with an image of his mother with whom he wanted intimate closeness. He turned away from the pastor toward his representation of his mother in an attempt to avoid feeling the intolerable anxiety of rejection. His response was also an expression of how he felt toward the pastor and what John really wanted, that is, greater closeness.

John's feelings of rejection from the pastor were associated with the rejection he experienced from his mother. But this image of his mother to whom he turned was embedded in an interpersonal relationship that could only hurt him more. John's representation was of a mother who was angry, unempathic, and who rejected him in favor of other people. John felt utterly and tragically separated from his mother, and through his current interpersonal relationships, he was constantly trying to find ways to be reunited with this childhood representation of mother.

John also recalled the image of his father. This representation was of a father who was unable to discover the truth, namely, that John really did intend to poison his brother. John also blamed his father for leaving him when the rest of the family went to the hospital. In John's eyes these two "facts" made his father impotent. Impotence was an interesting quality to ascribe to his father; he could have chosen, for example, ignorance. But at the time of this trauma, John was five. He not only had to compete with his brothers for his mother's limited attention, but he had to compete also with his father. In some respects, representing his father as impotent gave John a partial Oedipal victory, if only in fantasy. In John's eyes John had proved himself more powerful than his father by keeping a secret. Hiding his big secret, in John's mind, was like hiding his father's big penis. He also projected his own feelings of being "put out" by his mother onto his father. John, as an adult, always found himself looking for this childhood mother and father. One of the results, however, was that when John found such persons, he felt like a five-year-old. Thus John constantly felt rejected, belittled, impotent, and angry toward those he loved.

Yet, interestingly enough, John found solace in these feelings of rejection, anger, etc. As painful as they were, they also enabled him to identify with his parents, that is, to be what he thought an adult ought to be. These feelings were also preferable to his feelings of guilt. In order to avoid the pain surrounding these guilt feelings, John repressed them; that is, he rejected them as part of himself altogether. But when these painful feelings stirred within him,

John reacted with extreme anxiety, because the integrity of his self was at stake.

Every time John felt misunderstood by the pastor, he related a memory, usually one containing an image of a significant person. The pastor made a mental note of when these empathic failures occurred and the evoked images. Thus the pastor and John benefited from the pastor's small failures. The failures were redeemed, so to speak.

The pastor never had to try to fail to understand, because failing is a part of being human. Accepting empathic failures as inevitable suggests an objectivity about oneself. Over time John learned to accept that the pastor was not perfect. John found himself forgiving and being less angry. He slowly began to let go of the childhood representations of his parents because he finally found an appropriately empathic object in the pastor. In so doing he gained a new objectivity about himself, and he no longer had so much psychological investment in being impotent. John was no longer condemned to repeat the past but was free to create a more self-fulfilling future.

The caregiver does not have to try to fail to be empathic. That happens from living a day-to-day existence. But this does not mean that the caregiver should fail to such an extent that it traumatizes the careseeker. Traumatic empathic failure only makes a person more defensive and harder to reach. I once had a client who was trying to integrate her sexuality into her sense of identity. She always found herself choosing men who abused her. The patterns displayed by this client did not make sense, and I found it a very frustrating case until she finally shared what had happened to her while she was seeing another therapist. Although that therapy had occurred more than five years before we began, she recalled it vividly. Upon several occasions, the former therapist had openly suggested that her father had sexually abused her. Athough she had no memory of any such abuse, she found herself in doubt about everything in general and her sexuality in particular. She thought perhaps she had just forgotten or repressed her memories. While there was much more involved in her sexual problems than her therapist's empathic failure, the fact remains that this therapist had traumatized the client and moved her sexuality problems further beyond our reach.

The Importance of Valuing

The caregiver also wants to know how the careseeker protects and defends what is valuable to him or her psychologically, that is, what matters the most, what motivates, what inspires. Because John came to the pastor for counseling in part to understand how God healed him and then seemingly allowed his pain to return, the pastor suspected that God would be an important issue in counseling.

The pastor had an understanding of how it was for John to be John here and now. John had a growing sense of clarity about himself and greater objectivity. These gains helped give John the courage to proceed. From their time together, the pastor began to see that John had never been much in his own eyes. He was still a frightened, hurt, and guilty little boy much of the time, but even that was better than being nothing. Nothingness was John's alternative to being that little boy.

Either John was nothing or he was that little boy. This means that any time John felt intolerable anxiety—that is, when he felt he would cease being a self, or "go up in smoke"—he had the choice of being nothing or being that little five-year-old boy. The first part of therapy dealt with what it meant to be that little boy with the pastor. The subsequent phase moved into greater interpersonal depth, that is, understanding the intolerable anxiety of "going up in smoke."

John's case is an illustration, not a prescription, of how caregiving ought to proceed. What is important is the method, the questions, the empathic approach the pastor uses. The order of revelations about John's inner world are not necessarily important.

A Criterion for Proceeding "Well"

A caregiver knows the counseling is going well if the interpersonal relationship is *generally* going in the direction of greater depth and scope, a phrase and criterion first used by psychiatrist Harry S. Sullivan. The relationship does not proceed, however, without occasional retreats from interpersonal intimacy. Empathic failures decrease the depth and restrict the scope of the relationship, because they raise the careseeker's anxiety, but they are necessary if the careseeker wants to live in a world with other people. What the careseeker needs is greater insight and resources to find some degree of self-fulfillment despite the inevitable failings of other people. The caregiver invites the careseeker to use empathic failures as signposts or temporary campsites along the way toward greater interpersonal intimacy. Empathic failures may be resting points or indications of detours, but they do not have to be the end of an interpersonal relationship. They "mark the trail" of persons traveling together. In the case of caregiving, they may mark the way of two persons, bound by trust, journeying toward holy ground.

Yearning for Interpersonal Intimacy

For John empathic failure was like the window in his memory of his mother nursing his baby brother. It kept him from his mother, but it also protected him from merger and dissolution into his mother. John longed for reunion with his mother but was fearful of what it would mean, the destruction of himself. The image of a window symbolized his wish to be with his mother and his fear of being with her. Hence John craved empathy, but he dreaded it.

A repeated nightmare was associated with John's anxiety toward his mother. In the nightmare, John was drowning in a dark, murky, bottomless sea. The sea, as John understood it, was a vivid image of his mother as engulfing; it also related to his own feelings toward his wife being a mother. His wish of having his mother was tempered by his fear of what it would mean to have his wish come true. Being close to his mother would mean she would "know" John's secrets or worse still that she might tell his father. Hence, keeping his mother "in the dark" was a way of distancing himself from his mother and keeping his father powerless. If John was "found out," he feared that he would be punished for the horrible "crimes" he had committed.

John's childhood wish was for interpersonal intimacy with his parents, but the imagined cost was a "punishment" too great to bear. John imagined his mother would "kill" him and that he deserved it. So John felt he had no alternative but to remain guilty, unpunished, and utterly cut off from both mother and father. John never quite gave up hope that he might find the intimacy he craved, yet he was surprised when he found it: he held his wife in very high regard. But the closer John felt to his wife, the more he depended on her, and then the more anxiety and conflict he felt. Consequently, John vacillated between being very close to his wife and very distant, feeling anxious all the while. When asked about Judith's response to his vacillations, John said, "At first she thought she provoked my distancing, then she got angry. Now she leaves me alone, and I am becoming a smaller and smaller part of her life."

The pastor then brought the conversation into the present, "How is it different with me?" John replied, "Oh, you have to be here." Then he added slyly, "You need me to keep some of the church programs going." "In other words, I can't leave you," the pastor said. "You got it." The pastor left that session shaking his head.

Object Relations Theory

Once a caregiver gains entry into the careseeker's inner world via empathy, how is the caregiver to understand what is found? We have already noted the importance of empathy and of looking for patterns, especially the recall of particular memories when the careseeker experiences empathic failure from the caregiver. A person's inner world contains representations of objects, including representations of the self as an object of soothing, for example. To reiterate, the term *object* means other people and other areas of human interest outside the individual. "Objects," then, can describe not just other humans but animals, pets, or interests pursued, such as music, literature, or whatever. Health, viewed in this context, is measured by the degree to which a person is capable of unencumbered, variegated, profound, intense interest in objects.

In object relations theory, object-representation is one particular case of more encompassing processes. These processes are representing, remembering, fantasizing, interpreting, and integrating experiences through defensive and adaptive maneuvers. These processes occur within and as a result of an interpersonal context. As two people interrelate at a particular time, the processes of representing, remembering, fantasizing, interpreting, and integrating intertwine to form a representation of each person. After an encounter with an object, the interpersonal relationship as experienced by the person becomes part of the memory processes. The memories are then codified, stored, and regulated. Aspects of the experience are weighted, colored, or otherwise marked with special significance. The mind makes some aspects of the interpersonal encounter available for retrieval. Note that representations of objects necessarily include the interpersonal context.

In a real sense, one can never represent an object without in some way representing the interpersonal context. Part of the interpersonal context is necessarily a personal sense of being oneself within the context. Hence, part of an object-representation is a self-representation as relating to that object at that time. Likewise, object-representations are formed in accordance with the prevailing defenses and adaptations necessary to maintain a particular sense of self. Simply stated, one can never see another without seeing some aspect of oneself. One can never remember another without experiencing to some degree what it was like to be oneself with the object. If one uses a foreground/background metaphor to express this thought, an object-representation in the foreground has as part of the background a representation of the self. A representation of the self in the foreground has as part of the background a representation of an object.

The Developmental Nature of Representations

The process of representing objects and the self forms the matrix of human experience. This process is also developmental. Hence when exchanges with others occur they are remembered in ways that correspond to a person's developmental level. The particular developmental level influences both what is remembered about an interpersonal exchange and how it is remembered.

Any relationship to an object necessarily entails the whole developmental history of the person with similar objects. Any memory of an object will depend upon the nature and pattern of exchanges with the object, the current memories of the object, and the capacity to represent the object available to the person at the time when various exchanges occurred with the object.

Here is an example. When Alvan felt depressed, he pictured himself again sitting in his sixth-grade classroom. In this classroom he was surrounded by other students who laughed at him because he was a "nerd." This memory confirmed his self-image as a social outcast who was lonely, the butt of jokes, and sexually unattractive. In many respects Alvan remained stuck in the sixth grade. This memory of being hurt and ridiculed by his classmates is a visual yet nonhallucinatory memory. For Alvan, his current coworkers, the adult counterparts to his classmates, were always a little suspect. He believed they would not pass up an opportunity to ridicule his work. Needless to say, Alvan was paranoid about his coworkers talking about him. Likewise Alvan took a long time to trust his counselor.

John could still picture being "put out" by his mother and the tragic consequences of telling his brother that the kerosene was really water he could drink. In many ways, John had remained this five-year-old, for whom being "put out" had a literal meaning. The literal meaning was seemingly confirmed to John when he was "left out" as the family drove to the hospital. For John there was another related feeling, although the meaning of this feeling did not become clear until much later in his therapy. Being "put out" also referred to a feeling of being smothered. During these times John was unable to catch his breath. This feeling of being smothered was a way John remembered his intense desire to feel the closeness of his mother's breast and his intense fear of being too close. As a result John's feelings about sex and his capacity to enjoy sexual intimacy were distorted.

The Integration Process

A person is the subject of his or her experience. He or she has a synthetic capacity to order experience according to subjective significance and meaning. It is interesting to note how John's younger brother understood the "kerosene incident." John reported this memory to illustrate how different he and his brother were, even at ages five and three. According to John, his brother's recollection was vivid but sketchy. The brother remembered being held by his mother as his father drove to the hospital. He also remembered his mother standing by him as the doctor pumped his stomach. To John's dismay, because of that incident his mother and brother became closer. As a result of the same event, John experienced his mother as abandoning him while his brother felt a new closeness to her.

Different memories associated with the same object become integrated. Sometimes certain memories such as childhood memories are ascribed meaning later and are integrated in various ways. For example, John ascribed to the memory that his brother felt closeness to his mother the added meaning that she loved his brother more than him.

Conflict in Object-Representation

A person's object-representations change. In many ways the changes parallel psychological development. As a person matures or gains new experience with objects, the way he or she integrates those object-representations may also change. If object-representations change, there may be differences, and where differences occur, there is the potential for conflict.

Some representations may conflict with other representations. That is, a person can never remember another without remembering, to some degree, what it was like to be a self with that other. What may be in conflict is not only the newly elaborated self with the object, but the newly elaborated self with the self-representation that inadvertently accompanies the object. In other words, the self I am with this object conflicts with the self I now feel myself to be. To integrate conflicting senses of self, the person also has to reinterpret the object. But if the object is too anxiety provoking, the person may not be able to integrate the conflicting senses of self. The anxiety of living with conflictual senses of self may be less painful and therefore preferable to reinterpreting the object. What happens then is that in addition to avoiding issues surrounding the object, the person may also have to avoid dealing with issues surrounding the conflicting self-representations.

John clearly played out this scenario. This may also help explain why part of John remained five years old. John could never remember his mother without remembering to some degree what it was like for him to be "put out" by her. Tragically, this sense of rejection became a predominant feature of their relationship even as John matured. Every time John's mother hurt him, he felt in some way as he did that day when he was five—hurt and rejected. Likewise, these same intense feelings recalled images of himself wanting intimacy yet fearing the dependence he associated with it. John inevitably matured, and as he did, he experienced himself in new ways. Yet he could never reconcile the image of himself as strong and independent with the deeply embedded image of himself as weak and dependent. John's "solution" was in part his identification with the castrated father. Hence John had a lot of psychological investment in being impotent.

When John married he saw himself as a strong and independent man. Judith was seemingly attracted to him for these personal qualities. But as his relationship with Judith deepened, he found himself becoming more dependent on her. On one hand, his dependence seemed to enhance Judith's own sense of self-esteem, but on the other, John's growing dependence provoked in John deep anxieties of being rejected. So John saw himself caught between pleasing Judith and fearing her rejection. He also saw himself caught between feeding his own sense of independence by taking care of her, and becoming more dependent on her the more he took care of her because he felt closer to her.

Because John's anxieties about being rejected were closely associated with his feelings of dependence, John deeply resented Judith's desire for children, whom John saw as competitors for Judith's love. Here again he was caught between his images of himself as strong and independent and as weak and dependent. So John outwardly complied with Judith's desire to have children and inwardly harbored feelings of rejection and hurt.

Anxiety and Integration

As people experience new and different representations they integrate or fit them together into some kind of cohesion. Thus representations grow in complexity and subtlety as persons mature. One manifestation of this is that as persons mature, they no longer see persons or issues strictly in "black or white." The more integration that takes place, the more subtlety in coloration one sees. Considered from one angle with one set of assumptions, an object looks one way. Considered from another, the same object looks another.

No one, however, ever achieves completely integrated objects. What prevents integration? Simply put, anxiety. Anxiety is the antithesis of integration. According to Sullivan, anxiety is a disjunctive, disintegrative tendency that skews interpersonal relationships. At the very least, anxiety clouds awareness and at the most totally blinds people to their surroundings, including their own inner sense of self and other.

Anxiety may hinder or prevent integration, but it may also cause errors in integration. Anxiety clouds awareness as fog obscures a driver's view of the road. Because a driver cannot see the road clearly, he or she might wander into the oncoming lane of traffic. If the driver stays in the wrong lane too long, an accident is sure to occur. The same is true for a person who relates to others with a view obscured by anxiety. Other people's innocent remarks may be transformed into hurtful jibes. This was the case for Alvan, who could not accept that his coworkers had no sinister motivation when talking about him.

Other Factors in Object-Representation

Different object-representations result from different types of experiences. That is, other patterns in a person's psychic life impact the formation of object-representations. These include perceptual memories, defensive distortions, sexual or aggressive wishes, transformations, and modifications precipitated by the developing sense of self. This means that the prevailing status of the mind affects object-representation. Hence when we remember an object we also recall, in part, our mental status at the time we represented the object.

An object-representation includes not just what kind of exchange took place between self and object, how it felt, what developmental level was operative, and so on, but also what should have, could have, and ought to have occurred in the exchange. For example, an object-representation of one's father could include elements of the real father as experienced, the feared father, the wished-for father, the need-satisfying father, and those elements of the father that are too anxiety provoking to be remembered. An object-representation of God might include God as experienced, the feared God, the wished-for God, the need-satisfying God, and those elements of God that are too anxiety provoking to be remembered.

Defensive Processes

In the Freudian tradition, defensive processes are those unconscious activities which interfere with memory processes. These activities include repression.

Repression prevents or protects a person from being fully aware of who she or he is and the past from whence that person comes. If there is massive repression of an object- or self-representation, the person may experience loneliness, emptiness, or debilitating feelings of abandonment or loss. Massive repression and other defensive maneuvering can make life so uncomfortable or painful for a person that the give-and-take of everyday relationships is rendered impossible, with no hope for future relationships.

Defensive processes can prevent persons from entering into new relationships of any appreciable depth or scope due to the pain of simply being with another person. Some careseekers describe this feeling of pain using the metaphor of a hole.

Jane, a pastoral counseling client, felt her hole keenly. Jane was traumatized at the age of four by witnessing the death of her father. From ages twelve to seventeen she was sexually abused by her stepfather. She was terrified because this hole would change sizes uncontrollably. Jane was especially afraid to go to sleep at night. Through therapy she decided that she could control the hole if she could find its dimensions, that is, if she could find where it stopped and where it began. During times of extreme anxiety she would go on a frantic search for something that could plug up the hole. Often she chose a penis. Her promiscuity caused her a lot of guilt, but guilt was preferable to the panic caused by the gaping hole. She felt that if the hole got too big, she would fall in and disappear. Jane imaged hell as falling forever, and heaven as a place where one would feel one's feet firmly on the ground.

Rizzuto suggests that memories that contradict a person's needs, wishes, or prevailing self-representation come to consciousness when the person tries to deal with aspects of the self historically linked with the original object. Jane's need for love and companionship was constantly contradicted and confused when she tried to deal with memories of her stepfather, particularly the sexual aspects of the relationship. Jane had trouble separating her need for male friends and companions, her desire for satisfying sex, and her wish for reliable, nonsexual care from her stepfather. For Jane to trust anyone, she had to tolerate a lot of anxiety. Trusting anyone, male or female, meant that they had to walk to the edge of the terrifying hole. Jane feared that they too might fall in. She even fantasized that she might push them in to appease the hole's voracious appetite.

Jane illustrates in a powerful way what a profound effect an object-representation may have and how it can affect the daily living of a person. In Jane's case the object-representations of both her dead father and her stepfather, who she wished was dead, were powerful forces that shaped her life.

The representation of the dead but longed-for father both sustained her through times of her sexual abuse and yet created a psychological environment where Jane was more easily victimized by her stepfather. Amazing to her counselor, however, was how well Jane functioned in her everyday life, given the amount of anxiety she carried. Despite the panic she often felt, she managed to go to work most days.

Rizzuto also makes the point that an inability to settle a problem with a conflictual object, in Jane's case her father(s), may affect a person's life almost as much as the actual object had done in the past. Jane also exemplifies this point. Jane kept the conflictual object of her father alive in memory no matter how she wished the object dead and gone. Toward the end of therapy, Jane came to terms with the fact that although she had been victimized and was not responsible for her stepfather's actual abuse toward her, she could be responsible for not being victimized by her own behavior.

John also used the metaphor of a hole to describe his unbearable emptiness. During one session John began talking about his half-hearted attempts to quit smoking. As John talked, the pastor observed that John was expressing fear, especially when John mentioned Judith's displeasure with his failures to quit. As John continued talking about quitting, the pastor noted a knot in his own stomach that seemed to come and go. The pastor knew that this knot was symptomatic of his own feelings of fear. The pastor asked John what he was feeling as he talked. At first John denied having any feeling, but as he focused within himself he began to experience intense fear. As the feeling intensified, John reached for a cigarette. He began to inhale the smoke deeply. As he did this, the fear subsided in John and the pastor's knot went away. John also changed the subject. The pastor made a mental note of John's anxiety about talking about this feeling of fear and his attempt to quell it. The pastor made an attempt to refocus John on his feelings, but John again changed the subject. So the pastor simply stated that John had changed the subject rather than talk about his feelings of fear.

During the following session, the pastor again noted that familiar knot in his stomach. This time the feeling surfaced while John was talking about his mother. In this memory the mother was nagging John about not doing his homework. John smiled as he talked, noting how silly his mother seemed at those times, but the pastor noticed that he felt the knot tighten in his stomach while John smiled. John began to reach for a cigarette. The pastor asked John to wait and instead focus on his feelings. John became increasingly uncomfortable. The pastor again asked John to resist the urge to smoke and instead concentrate on his feelings. Suddenly John began to cry. As John cried, the pastor felt deep sadness. John said he felt like he was inside a hole. It was dark and he was afraid.

The pastor asked John to focus on that hole. With great difficulty John spoke about his feelings of despair. As John talked, the pastor noted the knot in his own stomach began to subside. After a long silence between the two of them, John expressed thanks and said that no one had ever been there with him before.

The pastor felt his own eyes fill with tears; his own mixed feelings included sorrow but also a sense of pride in John. John said that he finally had let somebody "in." It felt uncomfortable but also good somehow. The pastor asked if John still felt the urge to smoke. "No, not now."

This experience of being with John inside that hole confirmed to the pastor that he had indeed gained entry into John's inner world as a trusted presence. For the pastor it was a sign of hope that the counseling process was headed in the direction of greater depth and scope. For John it was a sign that there was hope he might get better.

Shoring Up the Self

Entry into a careseeker's world can be understood theologically as a manifestation of hope. Psychologically, we may speak of it as a shoring up of the self. John used the pastor as a selfobject in order to repair his depleted sense of self. The term *selfobject* refers to a person's constructions of interpersonal experiences that are called upon to soothe, comfort, repair, and build up the self. When one feels anxious, shattered, torn apart, wounded to the quick, or, as in John's case, like one is falling into a bottomless hole, there is a means through self-experience through which one can put the self back together, "back on track," lick one's wounds, or, as in John's case, fill up the hole. This self-repair is achieved by using personal constructions of interpersonal experience, selfobjects. Kohut calls this self-repair "shoring up the self."

The idea that self-repair is a shoring up of the self is interesting. The word *shore* refers to the boundary between the land and sea: the coast. Perhaps by using "shore," Kohut implies that self-repair involves the self making a demarcation between self and other by drawing boundaries. But this seems to imply further that shoring up the self is a retreat from interpersonal relationships, an effort to tighten and reinforce personal defenses. Kohut means that shoring up the self, rather than being a retreat from interpersonal relationships into a defensive posture, entails being supported, propped up, and embraced by others. In shipbuilding, shores are beams that support or prop up the ship while it undergoes repair. In the counseling relationship, one indication that the careseeker uses the caregiver as a selfobject is that the careseeker draws closer to the caregiver during times of anxiety rather than retreating. In other words, during times of anxiety the careseeker may use the interpersonal relationship with the caregiver to decrease anxiety and to effect self-repair.

Cynthia, a twenty-eight-year-old, sought out a caregiver because, she said, she was thinking about a career change. What Cynthia really wanted was someone to help her overcome her lack of self-confidence. After about three months of meeting once a week, the counseling suddenly, so it seemed to the caregiver, took on a different character. The caring relationship was on a deeper, more intimate level. As the caregiver puzzled over what was happening, Cynthia misspoke. She said that "we" drew up her resumé. What she thought she said was, "I drew up my resumé." Later in the same session, as Cynthia was about to leave to go to a job interview, she said, "I guess we are ready to take the plunge." At the next session the caregiver pointed out Cynthia's substitution of "we" for "I." Cynthia said that she had been so nervous about the resumé and job interview following the counseling session that all she could think of was putting the counselor in her purse and taking the counselor with her. For some reason, Cynthia said, that made her feel less afraid. Cynthia had used her counselor as a selfobject.

In both examples, the counselor was physically present when used as a selfobject. This does not necessarily have to be the case. A person may call upon a memory to perform the same function. In John's case he usually recalled his wife or his mother, but both proved inadequate. Because his selfobjects failed him, John reached for an addictive substance to soothe his anxious self.

In contrast, when a selfobject is absent or unavailable, the person feels diminished. In some instances, a person may feel a state of painful or disorganizing emotional disequilibrium. Some people express a feeling of "coming apart at the seams," having "busted a gut," being "crushed," or having a "hole in one's heart." Whatever language a person uses, he or she suffers intense psychic pain. While some people use these phrases as metaphors to express their feelings, others mean them quite literally.

Object-Representations and Actual Objects

While we may, in some sense, "create the object we find," as therapist D. W. Winnicott suggests, our object-representations must have some correspondence to the actual object. There are, however, degrees of correspondence. Ego psychologist Heinz Hartmann's construct of "fit" is helpful: A person's object-representation may correspond to or fit the environment in varying degrees, and some fits are more adaptive than others. Some fits are too tight, unnecessarily constraining a person's behavior. Some fits are so loose that there are too few constraints on behavior. For example, a person believes she cannot touch anything red because it is dirty. When she touches it anyway, she rushes to the nearest bathroom to wash her hands. This person has too tight a fit. The other extreme is the person who touches everything and everybody, everywhere. This person has no grasp of social sanctions and consequences when it comes to touching. She has too few self-imposed limits or boundaries on her behavior. In our society, both are deemed pathological.

Some fits *are* better than others. What we may need is to borrow Winnicott's concept of "good enough." We need a fit that is good enough. A good-enough fit would be tight enough to be socially responsible and yet loose enough to afford a measure of personal freedom.

Some Counseling Goals

Helping a person fit into a world that can be shared is a goal of counseling. Seeing where one is, from whence one came, and toward what one is moving is helpful in finding a suitable place. The caregiver's goal is to facilitate more unobscured hindsight, clearer awareness of the present, and enhanced foresight. These are hallmarks of successful counseling. But another hallmark is a person's acceptance of what he or she does not like and cannot change. There are always pieces of a person's world, real or imagined, that just will not fit. As much as the careseeker and caregiver may want or even need to integrate, resolve, or master conflict, sometimes they must live with conflict that will not go away. For example, Ned could never fully understand why he remained married to a wife who had refused him sex for three years. He not only remained married to his wife, but he remained faithful to his wedding vows. Ned felt that his vows were made before God and therefore could not be broken "no matter what." As a result of counseling, Ned came to a deeper understanding of what it meant to him to be broken and how God was sustaining him in his broken marriage. Perhaps Ned would not be healed of his marriage, but he received a strength and peace that enabled him to endure.

Summing Up the Characteristics of Object-Representations

Object-representations are dynamic networks that can never be completely understood apart from their context. This context includes the interpersonal world of the past, the interpersonal world of the present, and imaginings of the future. The context also includes the person's defensive maneuvers, especially repression, and developmental level.

Object-representations are dynamic in the sense that they can be open to revision and reinterpretation. Within this characteristic lies the hope that revising and reinterpreting can be made in the direction of greater maturity and more satisfying living.

Object-representations correspond in various ways to the actual experience of the person. This means that object-representations have as a source the experiences of being with significant people in significant relationships.

Object-representations are not random packaging of interpersonal experiences. They correspond to reality in particular ways. They are based on the patterning of experience and are themselves patterned and interwoven into the mental life of the person. In this way, object-representations are understood as a structuring of experience.

2

Surveying Holy Ground

SILVIA CAME TO a pastoral counselor because she wanted a religious person to help her "get her life together." Silvia, twenty-four, had recently been apprehended by the police for "drunk driving" and assaulting the arresting officer. After a frightening night in jail, Silvia had appeared before a judge and somehow convinced the judge that what she needed was to "get right with God." She had assured the judge that God could prevent her from driving while drunk again. As part of her sentence, Silvia was required to see a pastoral counselor.

During the first two sessions, Silvia talked about how much she loved God. She believed that God already protected her and had prevented any injury to her when she drank. She tried to impress her counselor by saying how devout she was and how often she went to church.

Whenever there was a crisis in her life, Silvia talked a lot about God. When the crisis was over, she did not talk about God. It seemed that she had no further need for God. When Silvia became anxious during counseling, she would invoke an image of God. Silvia used this image to shield herself from her anxiety. Silvia seemed to use God as a shield in her interpersonal relationship with the counselor as well.

Silvia had grown up in an abusive home. Although she could not remember her father ever beating her, she could remember his violent rage. She remembered vividly her father breaking furniture and throwing things. Her younger brothers were beaten, but she was not. One day, when she was about seven, Silvia was alone with her father. He got angry and was about to hit her when her mother came in. Silvia's mother, who had never stopped her father from beating her brothers, or stopped her father from breaking things, now stopped her father from beating her. Silvia never forgot this, and she said that God must have had something to do with her mother standing up to her father, because her mother had just starting taking the children to church. After this incident, Silvia's father started going to church too.

Whenever she felt alone and afraid, whenever she felt threatened, Silvia prayed to God. She used God much as children use a teddy bear or another cherished thing, reaching for it when they are alone or frightened, or as they use particular ritual activities like singing "Jesus Loves Me" or reciting prayers.

Transitional Objects

According to Winnicott, these teddy bears or other cherished things or rituals are transitional objects. In infancy human beings begin to create and use transitional objects as a way to negotiate the inevitable psychic trauma of separation and subsequent individuation. With what Winnicott calls "good enough" mothering, a young child becomes able reliably to evoke the comforting, solacing presence of the mothering other. Through a relationship to either special things in the environment or through the use of particular ritual activities, the child experiences the comforting presence of the good-enough mother.

The quintessential characteristic of transitional object phenomena is that transitional objects are within what Winnicott calls an "intermediate sphere of experience." The infant experiences this sphere as neither wholly inside the infant nor outside the infant. Transitional objects are not part of the infant's body, yet they are not fully recognized as belonging to external reality. This bear is not part of my body, yet it is part of me. Whether a bear, blanket, or ritual, transitional objects are very special and highly cherished by the young child because they are chosen by the child to help get through times of impending separation from the mothering presence.

According to this line of thought, the young child matures and eventually gives up the transitional objects. Many parents have a story of how Sally gave her blanket to the new baby, or how Juan left his bottle at Aunt Ruth's house because he did not want it anymore. Yet the realm of the transitional sphere that is that which is neither wholly inside or outside the person, remains an important part of a person's life. Within this sphere people experience the arts, religion, imaginative living, and creative work. For object relations theorists such as Rizzuto, it is here that a person experiences his or her God. But the scope of the concept of transitional object is limited. It does not encompass peoples' experiences of the *personhood* of their God.

God and Transitional Objects

Silvia was referred to a pastoral counselor because she wanted a religious person to help her "get her life together." Whenever she felt alone, afraid, or that she was "coming apart," Silvia invoked her God. When the trouble was over, Silvia put God away, like putting a teddy bear back in the toy box. In many respects God represented the presence of her mother, especially during those times when she needed protection from someone she feared. Silvia used her God as a transitional object.

A transitional object is always a thing. It is something a person loves and cherishes. A child can love a teddy bear. A child can hug the bear while going to sleep. But the bear can never love the child back. The teddy bear can never throw its arms around the child and hold on tightly. However much a toy or song is loved, in the end it is still a thing. Only other people love back. To say that God may be used as a transitional object can aid our understanding of what God can be to someone, but if we want to further understand who God can be for that person, we must look for another concept.

Silvia used God like a cherished thing, something to be hugged when she felt alone and afraid. The problem was that Silvia also loved herself in much the same way. She thought of herself as something to be maneuvered, put "on hold," brought out only when it was safe. Silvia desperately needed her God to love her, because she thought no one else really could, not even herself. She did not want God to be just a shield between her and others. She wanted a God who would help her more intimately engage others. She wanted God or somebody to fill up the emptiness that alcohol could not.

Exploring Holy Ground

Chapter 1 centered on discovering holy ground. In this chapter I will focus more closely on exploring holy ground. Holy ground is where God and persons meet. The meeting is not one of casual acquaintance but of intimacy. For most people holy ground is also the place where the self is most vulnerable; that which is most holy to these people will therefore be well protected and defended. Approaching holy ground can involve enduring much anxiety. Exploring holy ground necessitates the accompaniment of a trusted companion, someone who mediates, facilitates, and sometimes introduces the person to his or her God. The caregiver's primary task is to provide an environment in which one is free to see the vulnerable or broken parts of oneself and celebrate one's strengths. This environment, ideally, is a place to see oneself as one truly is and to explore possibilities of who one can become. It is also a place to share who one is and who one is becoming.

What enables a caregiver to become that trusted companion? The caregiver must be able to do for the careseeker what he or she cannot do alone: accept the self as it is and contain the careseeker's anxiety.

"Accepting" in this context means that the caregiver can empathize even with the repressed aspects of the careseeker's self. These aspects of the self are so unacceptable to the careseeker that they have been relegated to the "not me" of the personality. "Containing" means that the caregiver can empathize with despairing, contradictory, or even irrational parts of the personality. These aspects of the personality are often in conflict with each other, for example, a kind, loving self-representation diametrically opposed to a vindictive, aggressive self-representation.

In chapter 1 I defined the term *selfobject*. In this chapter, I will show that the concept of selfobject can encompass peoples' God-representations. Using the concept of selfobject and understanding how a person uses selfobjects, we equip ourselves as caregivers to explore holy ground. Before we as caregivers can mediate, facilitate, or introduce God, we must have a clear understanding of who God is to the person or else she or he may not recognize God. We will not know what fears or expectations the person has about loving and being loved by that God. Silvia's story and other examples also illustrate a human need for a companion, someone who facilitates the exploration of holy ground.

Historically, many theologians have depicted God as a loving God who loves individuals. God is often portrayed as loving a person enough to initiate a relationship regardless of that person's feelings toward God. Many religious people consider the personhood of God as self-evident. But caregivers also know that who God is to the careseeker—that is, the dimensions of God's character or personality as understood by the careseeker—says a lot about a person's own sense of self. The concept of selfobject can guide caregivers toward a clearer understanding of who a person's God is and can be, thus enabling caregivers to be more empathic.

The Holding Environment and a Sending Forth

In current counseling literature the term *transitional object* has been explored extensively. The therapeutic frame itself is often thought of as a "holding environment," that is, an environment conducive to the formation and/or exploration of transitional objects. Seeing caregiving this way has given religious caregivers another way to appreciate the sanctity of caregiving. But, as most caregivers know, caregiving is much more than holding. It also involves, for example, sending forth. The caring relationship does often act as sanctuary, a place where the careseeker is free to experience his or her thoughts and feelings. But it must also prepare the careseeker to venture out. Ideally the careseeker also learns how to provide sanctuary, a "holding environment," for others.

Successful caregiving means that careseekers eventually leave, but when they leave, they take part of the therapeutic relationship with them. That is, they embody in some way what has transpired between themselves and the caregiver. In self-psychological terms, the careseeker gains greater capacity for empathy for both self and others. This enrichment comes as a direct result of the caregiver's empathy toward the careseeker.

Caregiving is about transformation of the careseeker's self, but it is not about living life totally absorbed in that which only satisfies "me." Extreme self-absorption is nonadaptive in any person. Interestingly enough, those who live self-absorbed lives are very limited in their ability to give empathy to or receive it from either the self or others.

Adaptive and Nonadaptive Narcissism

All relationships serve narcissistic purposes, but there is adaptive narcissism and nonadaptive narcissism. By narcissism, I mean self-love, but also one's sense of self-esteem. There is healthy, phase-appropriate narcissism and there is narcissism that needs healing. In fact, some of the most intense relationships to objects serve narcissistic purposes.

Silvia had a difficult time understanding how anyone could value her. For several sessions, the counselor simply listened and encouraged Silvia to express her thoughts and feelings. A bonding or connection gradually formed between the two. During one session Silvia began to talk about how being with the counselor was different from being "outside." "Here," she said, "I feel warm and safe. As funny as this may sound, I am enjoying getting to know myself. It's scary, too, but mostly it feels good. I think you must have something to do with it, but I'm not sure what. Most of the time, you just listen to me, but still you seem to care and understand me somehow." The counselor responded, "So you feel that I understand you somehow, and this both comforts you and scares you?" "Yes, I'm saying all of that, but what I really want to say to you is that *I* don't understand. I feel a lot better about myself, but why? And why does it embarrass me to tell you all this?" The counselor responded, "You're embarrassed?" "Yes, and a little angry. I don't like anyone to see me like this, but you must not be just anyone."

Silvia and her counselor had many such exchanges throughout their relationship as Silvia struggled with the mystery of what being cared for by her counselor meant to her. Who was this counselor anyway? Why did being with the counselor mean so much? Why was it so scary at times?

As Silvia forged a stronger and stronger tie to her counselor, the mystery of their relating only intensified. Silvia came to counseling for weeks feeling annoyed. Finally her counselor said, "You seem to be angry, and I think you've been angry for a while. What's this all about?" To the counselor's amazement, Silvia began to cry with long heaving sobs. Silvia cried for most of the session. Finally, Silvia said, "Ever since I told you how much you meant to me and I got embarrassed, I have felt terrible. You see me like I really am, and you still care. 'Why?' I ask myself over and over. I began to think there must be something wrong with you. Even when I close my eyes to go to sleep, I see your eyes looking back at me. Sometimes I just turn on the lights and try to escape by reading. But I finally got up enough courage to look more closely. There was nothing wrong with those eyes. Those eyes belong to you and not my mother. This is funny, too, but I could even see a reflection of me in your eyes. You know like when you look at someone sometimes? And then, if you really want to hear something weird, I remembered a scripture verse that my Sunday school teacher taught me as a kid. 'We see in a glass darkly, but then face to face.' "

From this revelation by Silvia, the caregiver began to understand that when Silvia felt anxiety she soothed herself by evoking the selfobject of her mother. Finding that the counselor was not mother both was comforting and scary for Silvia. This insight was accompanied by the memory of another selfobject, that of her Sunday school teacher.

The Mystery of Holy Ground

No counselor or therapist can deny the mystery of the healing that feeling understood can bring to careseekers. Standing on holy ground with a careseeker is an awesome and humbling experience. By holy ground, I mean that intimate point of contact between persons and their God. No one can ever stand on holy ground alone, because the essence of holiness involves being in relation to otherness, and, we hope, eventually divine otherness. We can never know who we really are without seeing our reflection in another's eyes, because we are easily blinded by our own fears and pain. We cannot stand and look fully into the glory of God; we can only exist in the light of God's reflected glory, but some people cannot even do that. They need the caregiver to redirect and refocus what is of ultimate worth and value to the self.

There is nothing magical in a caregiver's eyes, although some, like Silvia, might suggest or believe there is. But there is power in what they may mean to the careseeker: being understood despite of who one is or what one has done, being treated as a person of worth and value.

Too often, however, people mistake that which reflects God's glory for the divine itself. There is a great temptation for caregivers to believe that only they can facilitate a careseeker's adaptive change. Their means and methods are the only ones that count. There is the temptation for careseekers to deify the caregiver as the savior or devil who performed a miracle in their lives. It can be quite beguiling to a caregiver to be idolized, venerated, or worshiped. It is tempting for careseekers and caregivers to regard the caregiver's office, institution, or routine as sacred in and of itself, and not merely the gateway through which holy ground *might* be entered.

Kohut suggests that therapy is curative to the degree that the caregiver is empathic. I suggest that empathy is curative, in part, to the degree to which it reflects what is of ultimate worth and value to the person and that, over time, what is currently judged by the person as ultimate worth and value will gradually change as the person deepens and broadens his or her capacity for relationships.

Object Relations and Object Love

Object relations are not the same as object love. Some objects have nothing to do with loving other people but are in the service of narcissistic aims. In fact, some of the most intense relationships serve narcissistic purposes.

Martin was a handsome sixteen-year-old high school sophomore with low self-esteem. He sought out a counselor, because, he said, his girlfriend did not love him anymore. He sought out a pastoral counselor, because, he said, he could not afford a "real" psychologist.

Martin loved his girlfriend Sarah with all his passion and in all his fantasies. He was devastated when she did not return his feelings. As it turned out, Martin's primary modes of relating to Sarah were elation and devastation. Anytime Sarah showed any interest in him, he was elated. Anytime Sarah showed any interest in anything or anybody else, Martin was devastated or, as he said, "blown away." He was shocked that she could be interested in anything or anybody other than him. Martin was also upset and confused at his own feelings of emptiness when she was away from him. Somehow he sensed that she was a little too important to him.

Martin never did fully understand why Sarah "broke up" with him, but the counselor guessed that Sarah could not tolerate Martin's demands, and so she fled the relationship. Martin had had many girlfriends, but Sarah was special to him because she was a cheerleader. She represented his own success and popularity. Martin needed Sarah so that he could see himself as a powerful, sexually attractive man. He needed her so that he could see himself the way he wanted and needed to see himself. When Martin, who had ample financial resources, chose a pastoral counselor who charged relatively little money for counseling, it was an indication that Martin felt inadequate and impotent.

Although one could say that Martin's relationship with Sarah served narcissistic aims and that perhaps it needed healing, it was not altogether non-adaptive in his social circle. Although his failure with Sarah was painful, it made him feel like "everybody else." All Martin's friends wanted to date Sarah. The fact that she dated him at all was a sign that he was really somebody, only not as much of a somebody as he believed. Martin used Sarah as a selfobject. He loved her as a means through which he could love himself. Martin needed Sarah, another person, to love him back so that he could love himself.

A selfobject is usually, although not invariably, someone whom the person experiences as not fully separated from him- or herself. Some aspects of the interpersonal relationship with that selfobject person play a vital role in sustaining a sense of well-being, focus, and intactness of the self. Selfobjects originate in the intense human need for other people to confirm in the individual's own eyes his or her sense of being a person.

An Understanding of the Self

In order to explore holy ground within an interpersonal context, a caregiver must have a clear understanding of the self-in-relation. A selfobject is a person's own inner sense of his or her self-in-relation. A self is that cohesive and enduring sense of being an independent center of initiative and perception. Self-experience includes the awareness that "I am now here," "I am continuing through the here and now into the future," "I am aware of being aware," and paradoxically, a sense that "I am more than I now know myself to be."

According to self psychology there are three major parts of the self: the pole of ambitions, the pole of ideals, and the intermediate area of talents and skills.

Corresponding to each of these three major parts is a type of selfobject. Corresponding to the pole of ambitions are selfobjects who respond to, confirm, approve, and mirror the person's sense of greatness and perfection. Corresponding to the pole of ideals are selfobjects who the person can look up to and who will accept being idealized. Corresponding to the intermediate area of talents and skills are selfobjects who make themselves available for the reassuring experience of essential alikeness.

Empathic Resonance

Each of these three parts of the self has its own line of development, but in each case optimal development occurs within an interpersonal milieu of empathic resonance. By "empathic resonance" I mean a basic sense of being "in tune" with the other person. An interpersonal relationship that is in tune also connotes a sense of harmony. When an orchestra conductor tunes up the orchestra before a rehearsal or performance, each section of instruments tunes within itself and then finally the whole orchestra plays "concert A" together. If the orchestra is in tune, even the relatively untrained ear can tell. The conductor listens for and can feel the harmony. Waves of the A tone can be clearly heard. Great waves of sound are reinforced by the harmonic interaction of the various instruments. If the orchestra is not in tune, one can recognize the dissonance not so much by hearing it but by feeling the interruptions and disturbance in the wave pattern of the tone. Empathy, for our purposes, means an interpersonal milieu of order and harmony in which a person can experience a sense of harmony or wholeness within the self. Feeling whole contrasts to feeling diminished or empty.

If there is a rupture in the empathic environment, further development of the self will be distorted and damaged. The lack of appropriate empathic resonance from the person's selfobjects creates anxiety. The person fears that the selfobject will cease sustaining the boundaries of the self; that is, the selfobject will cease shoring up the self. Once the self is crippled, it continues to search for appropriately empathic selfobjects in order to soothe that part of the damaged self.

The person will search for selfobjects who will provide appropriate empathic responses at the developmental level when the damage to the self occurred. Here is an example used by Kohut to clarify this point: A mother picks up her baby. The baby feels herself part of the omnipotent strength and calmness of the idealized selfobject of mother. When the baby is ready, she walks away from her mother, but she will not go far without turning around and looking back at the mother's face. If she is an emotionally healthy child, sur-rounded by a milieu of emotionally healthy selfobjects, she will turn to look not because she is afraid and needs the reassurance that she can return to the mother, but rather to obtain the confirming reverberation of her mother's proud smile at her child's great achievement. The child looks for the "gleam in the mother's eye." This gleam signifies to the child the mother's pride and delight in the child's achievement. The pride and delight the mother commu-nicates in this instance is the phase-appropriate approval of an empathic self-object that confirms the child's sense of self.

But what if the mother reacts to her child not with joy and pride but with fear or even anger? What if her toddler's walking away usually brings anxiety to the mother? What if the child can never find the gleam in the mother's eye? These situations constitute a rupture in the empathic environment and a self-object failure. If there is habitual or traumatic rupture in the empathic envi-ronment, the child's self will be damaged and the child will develop into an adolescent and adult who will continue searching for that gleam she could never find as a toddler.

The Development of the Self

The self is a product of human development. According to self psychology there are five phases in development: an early formulation prior to age two, ages two to four, an Oedipal phase, latency, and maturity. The study of human psychological development is dynamic and often the site of volatile shifts of understanding. In this section I sketch an overall view of development that will be taken up in greater detail in the next chapter, in which I discuss a de-velopmental view of empathy.

People can become arrested in their emotional development just as they can in their spiritual or physical development. Traumatic selfobject failure condemns a person to search or quest for a lost part of the self. The tragedy is that a person searches as the self he or she was when the trauma occurred.

Here is an example. When Saul was about six, his parents divorced. Ac-cording to Saul, the upshot of the divorce was that he was left totally alone in an emotional sense. He felt abandoned and full of rage, but he did the best he could to avoid the pain of loneliness. He made up imaginary playmates. His imaginary playmates never failed or hurt him. He could make them come and go when he wished. The problem was that he grew to prefer his imaginary friends to real ones. While Saul was intellectually bright and received a uni-versity diploma, he was incredibly lonely. When his peers began to marry, again he felt abandoned. Again he was left with no one to "play" with. He could not enter into a significant relationship with a woman because he had closed off a significant part of his emotional self at age six. As Saul began to open that door to that part of himself through the help of his female therapist's empathic understanding, he found a little lost boy staring him in the face. The emotional attachment he felt for his therapist included the rage and intense love a six-year-old boy feels for his mother. Exploring holy ground with this man, in part, meant helping the man understand the child within.

Early Formulation

Because selfobject resonance and failure are phase appropriate to the developmental level of the self, it is necessary to have a general understanding of the development of the self and what selfobject resonance and failure look like in each phase.

An infant first exists as a virtual self; that is, the infant as an individual exists as a conceptualization of the family. The infant increasingly organizes individual experiences into categories of his or her own making, and as a toddler also reflects on his or her activities. The toddler often introduces his or her own categories by literally saying no to the parents.

Selfobject resonance at this phase includes a proud recognition by the parents that the toddler is a unique self. Selfobject failure includes a habitual fearful or anxious response to the toddler's increasingly independent sense of self.

Even prior to seven months of age, children experience appropriate response from their interpersonal environment. Their expectations of such response differ from those of more developmentally mature individuals; nevertheless, expectations exist. Many parents have had the experience of a two o'clock feeding, when the baby awakens an exhausted parent with loud crying. The parent picks up the still-crying baby and stumbles into the kitchen to get the bottle. As soon as the parent puts the bottle in the microwave, the baby stops crying. The baby knows food is on the way, and many babies know exactly how long it takes the microwave to heat the bottle, because if it takes a moment longer, the baby begins crying again.

Prior to age seven months age-appropriate response is mutual regulation. The very young infant represents this as a self-regulating other. This representation of the self-regulating other can be called a rudimentary selfobject. It is not a selfobject in the true sense of the word because the very young infant does not fully recognize appropriate response as empathy; instead there is mutual regulation, a component of empathy. But very young infants use their rudimentary selfobjects in attempts to shape what an empathic response is.

Mutual regulation takes place in an interpersonal context. Through the exchange of voices, gestures, facial expressions, gaze, and so on, a kind of mutual regulation of the level of excitation occurs. Parents often get intense satisfaction and joy from getting the infant to respond, and the infant can get extensive experience with self-regulation of his or her own level of excitation and with the regulation, through signals, of a responsive parent's level of stimulation.

Even the youngest infant can maintain or effectively cut off the interaction using gaze aversion. Exchanges of this type are an early coping function. That is, infants get experience with the parent as a regulator of their own levels of excitation. The parent becomes a means by which the infant regulates his or her self experience, and the infant uses the caregiver to pattern, organize, and control his or her own excitation.

During these playful interactions the infant experiences the peaks and valleys of emotion. Through exaggerated behaviors that are repeated with appropriate variation, self-with-other relationships become patterned. The patterning of these interactions becomes stereotypic or typical of what it means to be a self with the caregiving other, particularly when coping behaviors are needed. That is, these patterns are the same ones that are called upon for soothing, comforting, going to sleep, and awakening.

A word must be said about appropriate variation. There is no doubt that this is a characteristic of good-enough parenting. Appropriate variation in interaction means that there is enough flexibility in the interaction that novelty can surprise both the infant and the parent, but not so much flexibility that the infant cannot have reliable expectations from the interpersonal interaction. There must be enough constancy in the care-giving to allow the infant to find what is typical interaction. Obviously then, the infant needs the reliable presence of a primary caregiver who will be emotionally *intimate* with the infant in this way.

Because to soothe is a primary function of selfobjects, let us look at soothing in greater detail. An infant who needs soothing is often at an intense level of excitation, which may be perceived by the parent as a frantic cry for help. Many mothers and fathers who are primary caregivers can usually tell by the kind of crying the level of infant distress. It is as though the level of excitement has "run away" with the infant. The infant is beyond his or her own coping mechanisms. During such times it seems that the parent has to rescue the child from his or her own affect. How does the parent do this? By calming the infant down using what generally has calmed or soothed in the past. When holding a screaming baby, a parent does what is pragmatic, that is, what will work to stop the crying for the infant's benefit and for the parent's own.

If the parent does not exacerbate the situation, the parent can gradually bring the infant within the sphere of mutual regulation. Often the parent uses some kind of exaggerated behavior, repeated with appropriate variation. Such behaviors as rocking and saying what amounts to "There, there you're all right now" or "You are all right because Mommy's (or Daddy's) here" are often used. Note that soothing requires that the infant enter into a relationship, or there can be no mutual regulation.

This particular characteristic of soothing may be seen clinically in adult careseekers as well. Many years ago, I had a client who after the third visit phoned me at the office. He sounded upset, but as the conversation progressed he told me that he feigned the crisis. He just wanted to see what I sounded like over the phone, and if I could really calm him down in case there was an emergency. While many careseekers are not as deliberate as my former client, many come into the caregiver's office with a set of expectations of how the caregiver should and should not soothe them. Again, for soothing to take place, the careseeker must enter into relationship and accept the caring of the therapist, but often this is the very thing the careseeker cannot or will not do.

Mutual regulation does not mean that the parent and the infant or the careseeker and the caregiver regulate each other in equal amounts. Mutual does not mean equal. For example, parents bring much more history into the relationship, and the caregivers bring a theoretical perspective. But mutual regulation does mean that both persons, no matter how otherwise unequal, stand on some sort of common intersubjective ground.

Every week, Silvia came to her sessions after jogging five miles. In her mind jogging was part of the frame of therapy. It was the overture. While she jogged she fantasized talking to her caregiver and planned out her sessions, what she wanted and did not want to talk about. The caregiver did notice that Silvia was dressed in a warm-up suit every time they met, but he had no idea that she jogged exactly five miles before each session. Then one evening there was a rain storm. Silvia came into the office soaked. The caregiver made Silvia a cup of hot tea to warm her up. As she sipped, she sobbed. The storm had been so bad that she could not complete her five miles. It was at this point that Silvia turned to the therapist and made him *her* caregiver. Her own attempt at self-soothing failed because she could not complete her ritual. In order to create a new self-soothing ritual, she entered into a deeper relationship with the therapist through mutual regulation, and in so doing she was not only able to expand her repertoire of soothing behaviors, she was able to find new meaning in an interpersonal relationship. She found new meaning in talking face-to-face with the real caregiver, rather than performing what she had already rehearsed with the fantasized one. She was able to find a new dimension in her holy ground because she allowed a real person to stand with her.

Ages Two to Four

From ages two to four, children have fantastic dreams and fantasies of being the biggest and the most. Parents often see these fantasies portrayed in play. Children pretend they are the biggest and most powerful people they know. Many times this means that they play that they are mommy or daddy. Sometimes they play they are terrible monsters. Sometimes they behave like monsters, often to the parents' embarrassment. At other times these monsters enter children's dreams and become nightmares. At any rate, these grandiose and exhibitionistic imaginings establish the kernel of what will latter become full-blown ambitions.

Within the first few years of life, the child says, in effect, to the parents, "Look, I am here. I am me." This statement, whether communicated through acceptable or unacceptable behavior, is more than a demand for attention. It is the search by the child for the gleam in the parent's eye.

And it is the *parent's* eye the child needs. This gleam signifies to the child that "I really am here" and "I really am me." The child looks not only for recognition of his or her presence or being but for indications that his or her presence has value for the people who matter most: the mother and father. For the child, if his or her presence has value, the child's self has value to the child. The child says by exhibitionistic behavior not only "I am here " but "I am great." "I have worth," and perhaps at this level, "I am the embodiment of worth itself."

Out of the parents' understanding, interpersonal relationships emerge that will eventually lead to the recognition of the worth of others and the child's own self as an independent person. Between the ages of about two and four, the child especially needs the parents' mirroring. Mirroring confirms the acceptance of healthy exhibitionism as an indispensable foundation for the child's self-confidence. Generally a person's self-confidence is indicated by his or her ambitions. That is, the more self-confident a person is, the more ambitious the person will be. This means that the person has sufficiently high self-esteem to envision the self as an important person who achieves superior goals.

Gradually the child sees the parents and others as independent individuals, but until that time, the parents are an extension of the child's own system. Parents have no existence of their own. At this level of maturity the child believes that he or she has magical control over other people. But from these significant relationships emerge needed selfobjects. The child does not have the capacity to master all interpersonal situations. These selfobjects help the child make sense of affects and external realities that the child otherwise experiences as chaotic and threatening to the self. Selfobjects modulate, gradate, and contain affects. The omnipotence the child exhibits reflects fragility of the child's self and the child's dependence on his or her selfobject to interpret the world in an understandable way. The child, in effect, borrows the organizational capacities of selfobjects to understand what would be unfathomable without selfobjects.

For example, a mother took her two-year-old daughter, Beth, to the doctor for a checkup. The mother knew that at this visit Beth would get some regularly scheduled shots. The mother so anticipated and dreaded an upset child that she cleared the rest of the day. The mother fully expected Beth to be "impossible" because of the shots. Usually Beth really enjoyed visiting the doctor's office. The doctor had a fish tank that intrigued Beth, and the nurses never failed to admire how cute Beth was and how big she was getting to be. Needless to say, the attention pleased the mother as well. The visit went splendidly until it was time for the shots. The mother tried to smile but felt apprehensive. At first, Beth merely eyed the syringe. She apparently did not remember her last shot. To Beth the syringe looked interesting and she tried to grasp it. Then Beth looked at her mother and knew something was up. The moment Beth was distracted, the doctor administered the shot. Beth cried because it hurt, to be sure, but her mother heard something more in her cry. The mother heard a cry of anger as well as pain. Suddenly the mother realized that she was holding her own breath. The mother tried to relax a little, because she knew there was still one more shot to give. This time as Beth watched the doctor fill the syringe, she knew what would happen next, and she was afraid. Beth again looked to her mother who for some reason was doing nothing to help her. This time, however, the mother made a conscious effort to breathe regularly and said in a calm voice, "You are okay." Beth relaxed a little. The doctor administered the second shot and Beth cried again, but the mother did not hear the same degree of anger mixed with the pain.

Now, one could say that no one really knows all of what Beth felt, but one could never convince Beth's mother of that. The mother was certain she had communicated her own anxiety to Beth and that because she later had re-laxed, Beth had relaxed a little too.

From Beth and her mother's point of view a rupture in the empathic en-vironment occurred. Beth responded with cries of physical pain and with rage. The mother responded with anxiety. From Beth's point of view, people who usually delighted in her had hurt her. An environment that was usually safe became dangerous. Beth was bewildered by her mother's behavior. What is all this? What is happening? Mother signaled impending danger by a look and posture that communicated anxiety. The anxious look both warned and caused anxiety in Beth. Yet, in the midst of Beth's turmoil, she heard her mother's calming voice and saw a reassuring expression on her mother's face, despite the anxiety they both felt. Whatever was happening was tolerable. I am in pain, but I am not destroyed.

Although a rupture occurred in the empathic environment, Beth inter-preted it as manageable by using her mother as a selfobject. In other words, Beth used her mother to see, as in a mirror, what was going on. In a more limited way, Beth was able to merge with her mother's calmness. Beth knew that whatever happened she was all right because the situation was manage-able for her mother.

Just as people use selfobjects to make sense of unfathomable affects and interpersonal situations, they use selfobjects in other ways too. The young child needs and seeks approval of acts of independence, because these acts of independence are also attempts at self-definition. In fact, there may be some correlation between a child's self-definition and his or her sense of pride, a child's sense of personal significance and his or her self-confidence, and a child's active mastery and capacity for pleasure.

For the child between approximately two and four years, selfobjects re-spond and confirm the child's innate sense of greatness and perfection. But selfobjects represent interpersonal relationships. What greatness and perfec-tion come to mean to the child depend upon the interplay between the child and significant others. The behaviors that represent greatness and perfection are forged within the interpersonal matrix of relationship.

Selfobjects are not simply introjected parents; they are part of information-processing feedback systems. Selfobjects come about through interpersonal communication. Self psychologist Michael Basch says that these information-processing feedback systems are cycles that affectively weight the child's per-ception of the world. Interpersonal feedback sets the way the environment is perceived and further information is sorted.

"Affectively weighted" does not mean that affects are attached to information. Affects are not extraneous to the information received in interpersonal communication. Rather, affects shape the meaning of the experience relative to other experiences. Affects are part of a person's perceptual apparatus that strains future experience as does a sieve.

This complicated interplay with the selfobject is mirroring. Mirroring is a kind of interpersonal conversation. In the above example, Beth saw not only her mother's anxious look but an expression of her own. When Beth saw calmness in her mother's face, she could experience her own. But at the same time, the mother saw her own fears portrayed in the face of her baby. The mother could more easily relax when she saw her baby's fear relieved.

A child's sense of innate greatness and perfection in handling "impossible" situations is always tempered by selfobject responses. What ends up being greatness and perfection to the child becomes the baseline of all further measures. The sense of self and what the self can tolerate is experienced in this early relationship with an available selfobject, that is, selfobjects who shore up the child's self.

The Oedipal Child

The young child develops and masters the spoon and toilet, and then enters the Oedipal phase between the ages of four and six. Children in this phase delight in their own bodies. Not surprisingly, they are curious about bodies in general and their parents' in particular. Alongside this curiosity is an increasing awareness that perhaps there are people who do not consider the child all-powerful or perfect. The child has the dawning awareness that "Maybe I am not as powerful or perfect as I thought." This idea puzzles children until they find a solution. The usual and healthy solution is that they retain their godlike status by idealizing selfobjects. The child has available selfobjects with whom he or she can merge, thereby maintaining infallibility and omnipotence. Usually the child selects the most powerful parent, often the father, and then uses the idealized object as a selfobject to enhance self-esteem. Kohut says this kind of self-esteem becomes an organizer of learning, studying, talking, thinking, and self-observing.

Larry came to a pastoral counselor because he was having problems with women. He was a church professional, so he thought a pastoral counselor would offer him a "collegial" relationship; that is, be a friend but not ask too many questions. Larry grew up in what he described as "a house full of big women." His father, although loving, was often gone, leaving Larry at the "total mercy" of his mother and aunt. About the age of six, Larry had a religious experience and decided then and there to be a minister. Although Larry's mother was the most powerful person he knew, he idealized his father as he wished him to be, ever present and available, and named him God. Larry needed his God to be male in order to protect his vulnerable sense of being a male self. The problem for Larry was that as he grew older and began being sexually interested in women, intimacy with them (which was for Larry quite different from sex) still seemed far too dangerous. He desired women and enjoyed sex, but sex offered no fulfillment of his intimacy needs. Sex was a way Larry "vented" his frustrations.

Larry illustrates, among other things, that an idealized selfobject does not totally depend on the actual parent, but can be the wished-for parent. Larry did not choose the most powerful parent as he had experienced power, but as he wished that he could. Larry idealized his wished-for father in order to protect his blossoming sense of manhood. Larry's God had indeed saved him, but there was a price. Larry gave up the freedom to have interpersonal intimacy with women.

As Larry explored his holy ground, he found intimacy with his female caregiver. His feelings of closeness for her stirred his erotic fantasies. Larry first used his erotic feelings as a means to gain control over their interpersonal relationship. He tried to intimidate his counselor. The counselor guessed that Larry must be experiencing a great deal of anxiety. Rather than avoid talking about his fantasies for her, she encouraged him to explore what they meant. What thoughts and feelings were associated with his erotic feelings? First Larry talked about his shame and embarrassment for having these "sacrilegious" feelings for his counselor. During this series of sessions, he talked a lot about trust. As the trust between them deepened, memories began to emerge related to his intense yearning for his mother and extreme anger toward his father. As Larry talked about these memories of mother and father, he began to feel incredibly sad.

Gradually, Larry began to see himself differently. He also began to see God differently. In the first days of counseling, God was stern; now God cried with him. Interestingly enough, God's crying made God more powerful, not less. It made God much more available to hear Larry's prayers. It also made Larry more willing to listen for God's direction.

Gradually the child becomes aware that not only is he or she not a special repository for unfathomable greatness but neither are the parents. This awareness optimally comes through small, everyday, empathic failures. Disappointment and loss are the narcissistic dimensions of the Oedipal phase. The child, in effect, loses the idealized selfobject as an embodiment of perfection, because there has been a shift in the interpersonal relationship. The parents are no longer perfect in the eyes of the child. But the loss of the old familiar idealized selfobject is experienced by the child as losing a part of the self. If the losses and disappointments are small, only small parts of the self are lost at one time. If a child learns to manage small anxieties, the child can repair her or his self using new phase-appropriate selfobjects.

While self psychologists write about the child losing the idealized selfobject, not much, if any, attention is given to how that loss may feel to the parent. Parents may have a lot of narcissistic investment in being idealized by their children. Having an adoring child is the way some parents "prop up" their own self-esteem.

Stella went for counseling the same day her child went to a new school. She was concerned that he might not be able to adjust being away from her. She worried about the kind of influence those other children might have on him. In short, she was worried how she would adjust to being away from her child and that he might question her authority over him. It was as though she was concerned that she was losing an object through which she could admire herself as a "good" mother.

How the child and parents suffer through and come to understand these disappointments and losses determines whether the Oedipal phase yields to the next developmental phase or whether it becomes an Oedipal complex, that is, pathological. If parents respond to the child empathically with joy and pride at the child's increasing autonomy and independence, the Oedipal disappointments will have a healthy resolution. But if the parent responds with competition or inappropriate sexualized behavior toward the child, the inevitable Oedipal disappointments will become pathological, because there will be injury to the child's self.

Joy and pride of achievement on the part of parental selfobjects prevent the child's self from disintegrating into fragments of sexual impulses, and the child's assertiveness is not transformed into destructive hostility. The child reacts to parents out of love rather than out of fear. If the parents do not function appropriately as Oedipal selfobjects, the child will experience great anxiety.

But the Oedipal complex is ubiquitous, because no one lives in a totally empathic environment, and no one has parents who never feel envious of their children or respond with a degree of sexuality to their child's affection. All persons experience an Oedipal complex to some degree. But if a child lives with chronic selfobject failure, that child will proceed from occasional emotional imbalance to serious self-pathology.

In the above example, Larry developed an Oedipal complex because his father was largely unavailable to him as a selfobject. Larry idealized his father, but the continual loss of his father was too much for Larry to handle, so Larry substituted a fantasized father, God. Larry had to have a father as a selfobject to protect him from competition with his mother and sexualized aggression (as Larry perceived it) by his mother. But the fantasized father was an intrapsychic result of a meager interpersonal relationship with his real father. That relationship lacked depth and interpersonal closeness. Closeness with his mother was far too dangerous because it was too sexualized and potentially available. Thus, Larry created a father who would protect him from his mother and prevent Larry from inappropriately taking on his father's role. As a result, Larry split off his intimacy needs from his sexual needs, because the wished-for father, God, was created to meet his intimacy needs and protect him from his sexual needs. But a fantasy can never substitute for the real thing. Fantasized closeness cannot substitute for interpersonal closeness. Larry lived with serious self-pathology but, for the most part, he kept it under control by using his religiosity. As a minister, Larry was very concerned with the ritual of communion. Communion, for Larry, was a way to feel intimate with his God and yet atone for the guilt of what he perceived to be his excessive sexual appetite.

As a result of the Oedipal phase the idealized selfobjects become idealized goals. These goals are specific and related to the interpersonal context in which they were forged. In other words, goals are never fully devoid of the images, affects, and defensive maneuvers related to the interpersonal relationships that help spawn their psychic birth. To use a foreground-background metaphor, if goals are understood as foreground, a large part of the background is the idealized selfobjects. If a particular selfobject is taken as foreground, there will be particular goals in the background. Idealized goals are always affect laden and therefore never fully amenable to rational logic. What a goal means to the person and how valuable it is to the person depends in large measure on the idealized selfobject from which it was transformed.

Ellenor loved music and had a beautiful alto voice. When she felt anxious, she often sang hymns to calm herself. Her caregiver noticed, however, that she used the same language about her love of music and singing as she did her wish for a loving father. Ellenor's father was largely emotionally absent during her childhood. He worked two jobs to feed his large family. The times Ellenor felt closest to her father were those when she saw him singing in the church choir: to see her father for an uninterrupted hour was a real treat even if she had to share him with everybody else. Ellenor wished she could be closer to her father, but she had to settle for the front pew. From the front pew she could easily see her father and distinguish his tenor voice. She knew he was not singing to her, but for God, but that did not make her angry, so she said.

As Ellenor matured, she valued singing and wanted to choose a career in church music. Her fantasy was to be such a good director that her father would invite her to direct him as he sang a solo. She wanted her father to choose her over everybody, including God. But Ellenor also dreaded having her father's powerful voice aimed solely at her, so she never applied for any choir-directing jobs, although she said it remained one of her goals.

One could interpret Ellenor's dread in a number of ways, but I want to highlight that her goal of being successful in a church music career was related to her father as an idealized selfobject. Ellenor's dream of being successful in the church music business and directing choirs was a transformation of her wish to be with her unavailable father. She wanted to be a part of her idealized image of her father as the epitome of infallibility and omnipotence. As a child she realized that her father was not infallible or omnipotent or else he would have made them more financially secure. He was a failure as a businessman, even perhaps, as a father, but he could sing. Ellenor idealized this image of her father. It was this aspect of their interpersonal relationship that was transformed into an idealized goal of being in church music and the image of herself as a successful church musician. Ellenor idealized only a part of her interpersonal relationship with her father. She idealized him as a part-object. Moreover, this part-object was desexualized. The repercussions of this were tremendous. One consequence was that Ellenor was attracted to men who were conflicted with their own sexuality. She also found herself drawn to gay men.

The goal of church musician was then tinged with a dread Ellenor did not understand. She fretted, "Why can't I bring myself to apply for a directing job?" She had many of the necessary credentials. This was why Ellenor went into therapy, but it took many sessions before Ellenor understood her motivation for seeking therapy. Initially, Ellenor said that she was dissatisfied with her job and wanted to explore her career options. She intellectualized her dread. It took many sessions of exploring her holy ground before she found a way to understand both her attractions and repulsions for both her career goals and men.

What one dreads is related to what is holy to the self; that is, what one cannot fathom being a self without. As Ellenor reexperienced with her caregiver the relationship with her parents, and particularly her father, she came to understand how her career goals were inextricably bound to her relationship with her father. The anxiety brought about by the disappointment she felt toward her father tinged her career goals with dread of achieving the thing she most desired. Success as a professional church musician was her goal, marriage was another, but a desire for a loving relationship with her father and her fear of having one fueled her rage and frustrated her attempts to achieve her goals. Only after Ellenor, with a caregiver, sorted through the meaning of her relationship with her father as he was and as she wished he could be was she free enough to move on.

Interestingly enough, Ellenor projected the rage she felt toward her father onto God in order to protect her father and preserve him as an idealized self-object. (This was a prime reason she sought out a professional caregiver and not her minister. Her minister was too close to God somehow.) Eventually, she did this with her caregiver as well. Only when she could face her disappointment that her caregiver was not perfect could she face her anger. These insights came after months of empathic mirroring by the caregiver. As she ceased being angry with God, she experienced deep sorrow. But she was also free to feel worthy of love, first God's and then other people's.

Caregivers' primary task is to provide an empathic environment. Holy ground is God and persons meeting in this empathic environment. Persons are free to see broken or frail parts of themselves and celebrate their strengths. But it is also a place to be seen. Exposing one's weaknesses is akin to feeling naked. It is approached with much fear and trepidation. The purpose of care-giving is to create a space, a Garden of Eden *of sorts*, where a person can pursue lost wholeness. But finding wholeness understood as perfection is akin to finding the Holy Grail. This is only a fantasy, a wish. What persons find is that they can have joy, peace, patience, kindness, goodness, gentleness, self-control, faith, hope, and love despite brokenness within a caring community. The healing process moves persons toward wholeness. Healing may include living with scars. Typically persons also find that their scars can be "re-deemed" by providing empathy for others.

Latency

While development of the pole of ambitions is especially important between ages two and four, and while development of the pole of ideals is especially important during the Oedipal phase, development of the third pole of the self is especially important during latency. Latency is that phase of childhood commonly thought of as encompassing ages seven to about eleven. During latency the experiences of essential likeness, or twinship, foster further healthy development of the self. If there has been an injury to the self earlier in either the pole of ambitions or ideals, interpersonal experience can bring about a compensation. These psychic compensations do not cover the defects to the self as do defenses; they, rather, functionally rehabilitate the self by making up for earlier selfobject failures.

Kohut is not altogether clear on how selfobjects function in the experience of essential likeness except that they are forged in the interpersonal experience of working side by side. The concept of twinship as a third pole of the self was not developed until late in Kohut's life. In fact, the third pole makes its debut in Kohut's last major work, *How Does Analysis Cure?* which was published posthumously. The third pole is a theoretical refinement of the tension arc mentioned in earlier works. The term *tension arc* describes the flow of activity between the pole of ambitions and the pole of ideals. Kohut wrote and is often quoted as saying that an individual is driven by ambitions and led by ideals.

Perhaps the essence of twinship or selfobjects that shore up one's sense of alikeness can be expressed with the aid of Sullivan's notion of "chumship." For Sullivan chumship occurs during the preadolescent era of development. Chumship results from an intimate relationship with a significant other of comparable status, a peer. A chum is a person like me, of my own sex. An interpersonal relationship with a chum is like having a twin or another self. Most of the time it is a best friend or buddy who belongs to the same "gang." A chum is usually someone freely chosen as a friend, rather than a family member whose relationship is a given because of kinship.

Sullivan is talking about object love, to be sure. My point is that by being side-by-side, with a chum, for example, one can construct selfobjects through which one can love oneself.

In self psychology the notion of twinship is not limited to persons of the same sex or same age. But one does get the idea that twinship involves a peer relation, if only for a moment, or if only in the eyes and imagination of the child.

Silvia had vivid memories of this phase of her life. Especially significant was the memory of herself with her aunt working in the garden. She remembered with warm feelings how together they would set out pansies in the spring. Silvia recalled how they huddled side by side with their hands in the dirt. With great pride she recounted how beautiful they were. For Silvia, being with her aunt in this way was a comfort and a reminder that life could be beautiful even if one got one's hands dirty. "Getting one's hands dirty" became a way Silvia integrated her shame concerning her drinking problem.

This memory emerged rather late in the course of her counseling. Working with her aunt in the garden became a metaphor for her experience with her caregiver. As one might expect, "garden" came to symbolize her holy ground.

To summarize then: a person needs mirroring to facilitate the pole of ambitions, idealization to facilitate the pole of ideals, and experiences of being side-by-side to facilitate the pole of twinship. These three lines of narcissism intersect to form a cohesive and enduring configuration—the self.

The Mature Self

As anyone knows, the self is not mature after latency no matter how one defines latency. The self continues to develop probably throughout life, but the dimensions of this development are not yet fully understood. One thing is certain, however: people always have selfobject needs. These needs do not cease with maturity. Selfobjects are a necessary part of a life full of varied and sustained interests. Hopefully, selfobjects lead one to an awareness that the move from dependence to independence is impossible. The nature of interpersonal dependence may change, but independence from interpersonal relationships is impossible.

The mature self is characterized by five traits. (1) The mature person does not need to hurt an opponent unnecessarily, and aggression subsides when the goal in question is reached. This is opposed to the immature person who exhibits hatred and cruelty in the elimination of human obstacles to achieve a goal. (2) A mature person uses selfobjects to provide joy and fulfillment, not merely for the satisfaction of pleasure. Thus, needs are not merely satisfied and anxieties not merely blocked, but needs are fulfilled and given joyful, creative expression. (3) The mature person is increasingly objective vis-à-vis him- or herself and his or her problems. (4) The mature person experiences joyful pride and creative achievement in significant relationships. (5) The mature person can give empathic response to others without threatening his or her own capacity for self-soothing or his or her own sense of being a cohesive self.

These mature characteristics can occur because the person has gradually developed a cohesive structure, a self, using empathy and nontraumatic empathic failures. Gradual and nontraumatic failures are the result of failures of the selfobjects of childhood, which are no longer phase-appropriate. These failures occur when the available selfobject "just" misses being able to soothe the self. The self finds that it can repair itself using another available and phase-appropriate selfobject. Gradually the self builds a whole repertoire of phase-appropriate selfobjects that represent patterns of interpersonal relationships. Experiencing nontraumatic empathic failures encourages the person to seek alternate inner resources for self-soothing, thus broadening the repertoire of the self's capacity for holding the self together in the face of anxiety.

Kohut gives us an image of the mature person: "Tragic Man." Tragedy epitomizes the mature person. The tragedy of life lies in the person's empathic understanding of what being a human self means. This mature person realizes and accepts, often with despair, limitations—that is, the greater capacity one has for joy, the greater the pangs of despair, and that the more one fulfills one's ambitions, the more one realizes that dreams and goals can never be completely realized. Life is tragic because pain, suffering, and empathic failure are inevitable, yet they need not destroy the individual or the community. The courage to search for meaning despite what we believe is inevitable is an act of faith, and not just faith in or for the self but faith in and for others, including God. While there is tragedy in living, it too must be put in perspective.

The issues of tragedy and suffering are beyond the scope of this book, but every caregiver must have some grasp of the inevitable question: Why me, now? The caregiver may ask him- or herself this question as a methodological approach to careseekers, but suffering persons ask this question as part of their quest for meaning in the midst of pain. Tragedy can be put in perspective only if one believes in tragedy's redemption. Christians put the tragedy of the crucifixion in perspective by seeing it through the eyes of the Easter experience.

Psalm 51 says that God will not despise a broken and contrite heart, a heart that will not deny limitations or future possibilities. The psalm says that indeed a broken spirit is the sacrifice acceptable to God, because only then can God create a clean heart. A clean heart is one that is emptied of anxieties and fears and then filled by the power of an intimate encounter with God on holy ground. What are the results of meeting God on holy ground? They are the fruits of the Spirit. Galatians 5 lists them as love, joy, peace, patience, kindness, goodness, faithfulness, gentleness, and self-control. These fruits are not a magical potion against future conflicts, but they can offer grace to endure, power to sustain, a beacon to guide, hope to reconcile, and faith to heal.

Substitute Selfobjects

Kohut asserts that God is a hallucinatory product or substitute selfobject created using visual imagery when external reality is devoid of empathy. In a previous example, we saw how Larry created his God, in part, because his father was not an available selfobject. Larry's imagery was significant. For Larry God was so big that Larry could never see God's face. Larry's God sat on a throne surrounded by clouds. All Larry could ever see of his God was God's feet. Yet, even as an adult, evoking this image of God was comforting and imbued Larry with a sense of importance.

Self psychology sees the ability to create substitute selfobjects as important because these selfobjects can protect the self of the person from suffering permanent damage, especially during times of solitude. They can also provide the person with great strength and courage to perform acts that could not otherwise be performed without the aid of a supportive group or despite extreme social disapproval. In other words, some people, when they feel totally alone, can create a comforting presence that can protect and defend the vulnerable self. It is as though, when there is no apparent interpersonal relationship to draw upon, some people have the capacity to create one.

Two things must be said about substitute selfobjects however: the substitute selfobjects are not created *de novo*, and they may or may not have any correlation to the God of a particular faith. Images of God may have many sources, including parental introjects. Likewise even parental introjects are dynamic and have a developmental history within a person's life. Contrast your experience of being a child with a parent to your experience of being a parent with your child. The God of the faith community is the God of a historical tradition that has evolved and been reinterpreted over centuries. Not only that, but many faith communities would include in their dogma the notion that God is free to initiate interpersonal relationships as an independent actor, often despite humans' own desire or willingness.

As Silvia's relationship with her counselor increased in depth and scope, she became more comfortable with her holy ground. Before, fear had motivated her to put God back on the shelf when she was no longer in crisis. God was so dreadful and powerful that she felt unworthy in God's presence. As she gained inner strength, she was finally able to face her dread of her awesome God. One night Silvia had a dream in which she saw the face of Jesus smiling at her. A sense of peace filled her. As she related this dream to the counselor, they both realized that the face of Jesus had a changed character different from earlier in her therapy. And Silvia too seemed to be different. She was more accessible, more willing to engage her counselor.

Silvia's image of a smiling Jesus was a way to desexualize her unacceptable feelings for her counselor given the other attributes Silvia ascribed to Jesus. This suggests that the image constituted a resistance to further intimacy with the counselor. While this is probable Silvia also used the smiling Jesus as a selfobject in order to grow toward greater intimacy with the counselor. It may well be correct that Silvia integrated the empathy she experienced with her counselor with preexisting images to form this image of Jesus, but what is of greater importance is how Silvia changed in the process. She was more tolerant of anxiety brought about by interpersonal intimacy not only with her counselor but with others in her world.

While Silvia dreamed of the face of Jesus, not all images of the Holy are so easily recognizable. Some persons image a blinding light in a cave, some feel warmth, still others hear a still small voice. However it is experienced, the person has certain knowledge that he or she is not alone.

Twenty-year-old Sally went to see a caregiver because she was having problems with her parents. In counseling, Sally told how lonely she was as a child, partly because of her parents' strict prohibitions and partly because Sally herself was a shy, introspective person. Sally longed for a best friend, but more than that, she felt she needed a boyfriend to feel good about herself. One night, when Sally was about twelve, she felt empty and totally alone. A classmate had made fun of her at school; her boyfriend had "dumped" her. She stood looking out of her bedroom window into the night. In her desperate loneliness, she began to pray. She repeated a familiar Bible verse, "If God be for you, who can be against you?" She began thinking what it would be like to die, to just stop hurting if only for a little while. From deep within her came the realization that "it would pass." Her hurt, her parents' attitudes, her not having a boyfriend would not last forever. She continued praying and looking out the window for what seemed a long time. Suddenly, she felt surrounded by a warm glow. Sally said she felt as though she was inside a sphere that enveloped her whole body. She felt love, calmness, and peace. The strange thought flashed through her mind that she could breathe. Here, Sally thought, was God's warm embrace encircling her and showing her that everything would be all right. And Sally believed it. Everything for that moment was all right. Sally said that the warm glow faded and she was left looking out the window, but she was no longer lonely. She had faith that God was with her even though she could not feel him. Sally later said that in similar times of loneliness, she often tried to conjure up her experience with God, but she never could. Although Sally never again felt God in that same way, the memory of her encounter with God "sustained" her through some equally tough times.

For Sally, God was a selfobject. According to Kohut, the evoked image of God acted as a substitute selfobject, meaning that there were no tangible selfobjects, to call upon. This is only partly true; an image of God is much more than a mere substitution for parents who have empathically failed. The next chapter deals with the constitution of the image of God used as a selfobject.

Sally's experience with God was not a hallucination, although she described her experience with much visual imagery. She imaged being "enveloped in a sphere" and "encircled." In her recollection, the tactile references are also prominent. She felt "warm," "embraced," and the "arms of God" around her. In her vulnerable state, she had someone who shored up her self; someone who loved her by holding her together.

While Sally described her experience with God, her caregiver imagined an infant finding solace in her mother's arms, or safe retreat in her mother's womb, or refuge in a lover's embrace. Sally connected this event much later in counseling with a memory of her father. The key to her insight was the elusive phrase, "I can breathe." When Sally was about five years old, her father, in an uncharacteristic display of affection, hugged her with great joy. He had just come in from work. He still had on his raincoat. As Sally ran to meet him, he reached out with his hands still in his pockets so she found herself being hugged inside his coat. While she wanted a hug, she felt very uncomfortable. Inside her father's coat it was hot and she could not breathe. He released her laughing, intending nothing other than fun. He told Sally that even with the storm outside, inside everything was nice and warm. Out of his pocket, he then pulled a box from the bakery, a special treat. Sally gladly opened the box; it contained her favorite.

Sally's association between the incident with her father and her experience with God has a distinct Oedipal coloring. For Sally, the surprising and seemingly unimportant memory that within God's embrace she could breathe, distinguished her relationship with God and her father. On one hand, her father's strictness was suffocating her and stifling her growth as a young woman. God's love, on the other hand, was liberating and fulfilling.

Sally realized that her parents, particularly her father, did love her. But love to her father meant that he protected her by surrounding her with suffocating prohibitions that isolated her from potential friends, especially boyfriends. Sally's insight, in part, was her awareness that she could feel protected, inside an embrace, yet did not have to feel suffocated. Sally also realized that by loving her father, she did not have to be sexual like her mother; that is, she was free to be sexual in her own way. This complex realization carried with it the insight that some of Sally's Oedipal wounds, such as feeling that she had to sexually compete with her mother for her father's attention, were finally healed.

Sally's insights also extended to her parents' use of their religion as a barrier to separate themselves from other people. Sally decided that she could not and did not have to live within her parents' religious values.

For Sally, exploring holy ground meant finding connections between her relationship with her parents and her encounter with God. As she explored her interpersonal relationships, Sally's belief in God became stronger. She came to a new realization of who she was in relation to her parents and who she was in relation to God. The deeper her self-understanding, the more intimate her relation with God became. New awareness of herself gave Sally a sense of peace and a greater capacity to feel God's love.

Encounters with God, such as Sally's, raise questions for which self psychology offers few systematic answers. Where did Sally, or does anyone, get the capacity to create a substitute selfobject? Why can a substitute selfobject hold the threatened self together when a selfobject cannot? Why did Sally attribute her comforting to God only? Why not the caregiver? Why did Sally feel that her encounter with God was the most "real" thing that had ever happened to her? Why did her experience with God lead her to a deeper capacity to love and into an interpersonal relationship of greater scope with her caregiver? Why did recounting her experience with God still evoke strong feelings? Although Sally felt despair and utter loneliness again in her life, why did she have an encounter with God only once? How is it that Sally felt love from God?

Whatever the answers to these questions may be, one thing is certain, Sally used her experience with God in conjunction with counseling to solve some interpersonal conundrums. First, she forgave herself of her guilt for hating her parents, who, after all, were suffocating her, killing her, with their love. Second, she acknowledged that she had some responsibility to make and maintain friendships. Third, she saw that her parents were people with their own limitations, and that while they could not understand her as she wished, they loved her in their own way. Fourth, by understanding her parents in a deeper way, she strengthened her bond of love with them and yet felt she was a separate person. Fifth, Sally's self-esteem was greatly enhanced because she felt she had received the blessing of God's presence.

Sally's encounter with God was, in part, an adaptive use of a selfobject. It was not a flight away from reality but an experience of what was, for her, holy ground. It led her to seek out interpersonal relationships of greater depth and scope. It led her away from self-absorption toward a greater capacity to give and receive love and forgiveness from herself and others. It represented not a denial of her painful loneliness but an acknowledgment in order to cope with it. Exploring her holy ground gave Sally further insight into herself as a self-confident, better-integrated creation of God. Exploring holy ground enabled Sally to become increasingly aware of her own convictions, goals, and ideals, which she now felt free enough to pursue.

But a religious caregiver must also ask, Is an individual's God a substitute selfobject only? Is every encounter with God necessarily an adaptive experience? How can one segregate the pathological components from more adaptive components? What if exploring holy ground puts the person at odds with his or her faith community? What if exploring holy ground provokes intolerable anxiety?

Conclusions

For the caregiver, experiencing holy ground with a careseeker is a profound experience. While such an experience is not characteristic of all caregiving, the possibility is always there.

The quest for lost wholeness always entails steps of faith. The possibility of wholeness lures people in the direction of the Holy. Needless to say, no one will ever find complete or perfect wholeness. People may even find further conflict. But one thing is sure: if the self's relationships undergo transformation in the direction of greater depth and scope, so too will the relationship with God. By clarifying who God is and is not to the careseeker, the caregiver has a clearer grasp of the specific kinds of companionship for which the careseeker is asking, that is, what counts as a valued companion and what wholeness means.

Using the concept of selfobject from self psychology helps the caregiver understand *who* God is to the careseeker and ways that this God may enhance or hinder relationships. By clarifying who God is and is not to the careseeker, the caregiver can be more empathic in this area of the careseeker's life.

There are also methodological issues in exploring holy ground. When the careseeker feels shattered, the caregiver can observe how the careseeker soothes or shores up the self by being alert to what is currently happening in the room between him- or herself and the careseeker. What interpersonal relationship does the careseeker evoke from his or her memory in order to feel closer to the caregiver? Did the careseeker evoke God in order to feel closer to the caregiver? What interpersonal relationship does the careseeker evoke to avoid anxiety brought about by the closeness with the caregiver? The caregiver learns the pattern of the careseeker's turning toward, turning away, or even turning over and against in order to find the dimensions of empathy and empathic failure. Typically, a careseeker's images of God when used as a selfobject not only fit but typify the pattern of other selfobjects developed in childhood.

A careseeker also observes the kinds of memories, behaviors, gestures, fantasies, and vocal inflections that are associated with the careseeker's pattern of selfobject use. Only after much observation is empathic interpretation in order. The caregiver empathically interprets his or her observation to the careseeker and waits for response. If the interpretation is accepted, the relationship will deepen and extend in scope.

As the self's relationships undergo transformation, so too will that person's relationship with God. Often the empathy offered by the caregiver impacts the careseeker's image of God. In fact, if caregiving is optimal, or if cure is approached, this is expected. Despite the caregiver's limitations or even despite the caregiver's predilections, a caring relationship of increasing depth and scope will bring a careseeker closer to what is holy. And as the careseeker becomes more intimate with what is holy, there is greater wholeness.

— 3 —

Being Nourished on Holy Ground

TONY WAS A forty-year-old married man. He was a chemist at a pharmaceutical company. He initially went to his minister because he felt his faith "was just not working." The minister recognized some significant signs of depression and referred Tony to the local pastoral counseling center. At first Tony was reluctant to go, and he was angry that the minister thought there was something "wrong" with him. In fact, Tony did not call to set up an appointment for another three months.

Then one evening, Tony was in a car accident on his way home from work. No one was injured, but Tony refused to get out of bed for several days afterward. Tony's wife became increasingly worried and called their family physician. At church on Sunday, she spoke to the minister about Tony. Monday, the minister stopped by to visit.

The minister sat next to Tony for a long time saying nothing. Finally Tony interrupted the silence with an angry, "Well?" The minister met the force of Tony's anger with compassion and said, "What do you want me to say?" "You're going to say that I'm depressed and need to get help." "Are you?" asked the minister. Tony smirked and answered, "I'll call tomorrow." The minister picked up the phone beside the bed, dialed the number, and handed Tony the phone. "I think now is better." Tony reluctantly took the receiver and began his pilgrimage toward holy ground.

What precipitated Tony's call to the counseling center? Was it his initial conversation with the minister? Was it the car accident? Was it that his wife was worried? Was it the persistent compassion of the minister? As Tony and his caregiver explored these questions, Tony's recurring theme was that he felt a vague frustration with his life and his job in particular.

Tony was a kind, outgoing person. He was about fifty pounds overweight, but handsome. After listening to Tony for about three sessions, the counselor decided that Tony's distress could currently be contained by meeting twice weekly for psychotherapy. Tony agreed reluctantly. The counselor noted Tony's reluctance and asked what it might mean. At first, Tony denied feeling anything other than enthusiasm about counseling, but the counselor persisted that Tony did not sound very thrilled with the prospects of meeting. Then Tony said softly, "It's just hard for me to be here." There was an uncomfortable silence for several minutes. Tony finally continued, "I've never had to ask for help before." "You sound ashamed," responded the counselor. Tony's face turned red. "It's just hard."

The most important thing that goes on in the counseling room is the relationship between the caregiver and careseeker. As mentioned in the first chapter, one way to focus the relationship is for the caregiver to continually ask him- or herself, Why me, now? Another way to ask this question is, How is the careseeker experiencing my empathy, now? This question focuses the caregiver's awareness on the subjective or self-experience of the careseeker. The caregiver is seeking to understand how it feels for the careseeker to be a self in the here and now.

Asking "Why me, now?" is useful and necessary throughout the course of caregiving. It is essential to understand why this particular person is here with me in this particular context, telling me this just now. In Tony's case, he begrudgingly went to a pastoral counselor, despite his anger toward God. As the caregiver later learned, Tony's red face signaled not only shame and embarrassment but anger as well.

The "How is the careseeker experiencing my empathy, now?" question is also useful because it is a tool with which the careseeker achieves one of the most important goals of therapy: that over time the careseeker will gradually internalize the relationship with the caregiver in order to sustain or enhance a sense of well-being, focus, and coherence. In short, the caregiver becomes a selfobject.

To review: a selfobject refers to a person's construction of interpersonal experience that is called upon to shore up the self. A selfobject is usually, although not invariably, a person. Some aspects of the interpersonal relationship with the selfobject play a vital role in sustaining or enhancing in the self a sense of well-being, focus, and coherence. Selfobjects originate in the intense human need for empathic others to confirm and affirm each person's sense of being a person.

But what enables a person to construct a selfobject from interpersonal experience? What is it about a particular object that allows it to become a selfobject? Why does someone esteem an object so highly that she or he constructs an intrapsychic representation of it that can be called upon in times of anxiety? How can a caregiver facilitate selfobject formation? Simply put, an interpersonal relationship becomes the matrix from which selfobjects are formed through appropriate empathic response.

The curative effect of caregiving is achieved through the empathic caregiver who sustains selfobject experience and interprets inevitable empathic disruptions. These disruptions are a result of the caregiver's unavoidable, yet temporary and nontraumatic, empathic failures. The caregiver never has to try to fail the careseeker, because being human insures he or she will. When empathy fails in the here and now of the caregiving relationship, the careseeker may turn to a selfobject as a defense against anxiety. In other words, the person temporarily turns to a selfobject from whom empathy has been sought in the past. "Past" here has temporal and may have developmental dimensions. Hence the better the caregiver is able to be empathic, the better the careseeker can use the caregiver as a selfobject, and the more effective care will be.

In this chapter we will explore what appropriate developmental empathic response is. Understanding this will help the caregiver answer the question, How is this person experiencing my empathy now? If we know how someone experiences empathy, we have before us a means by which he or she can be nourished by interpersonal relationships. God is sometimes experienced as an immanently real, personal presence, as an evoked companion par excellence. It is with this kind of companionship that some careseekers seek to regain the lost wholeness of the self, hoping to be nourished on holy ground.

The Role of Empathy

Interpersonal relationships become internalized as selfobjects by giving developmentally phase-appropriate empathic response. But what exactly is an empathic response? Empathy is a methodological tool for the caregiver. It is a means by which the caregiver maintains what Kohut calls an "experience-near" perspective and from which the caregiver constructs his or her theory. Empathy is vicarious introspection. It is being immersed in the careseeker's experience while at the same time being aware of thoughts, feelings, or imaginings that resound in oneself. For example, as a careseeker remembers an incident in her abusive home and begins to feel sadness, the caregiver may experience sadness related to his own distance from his father. Or as a careseeker reminisces about returning to his childhood home, the caregiver may experience some longing and recall some childhood memories. But the difference in the empathy between a caregiver and careseeker, as opposed to between two friends, is that the caregiver remains focused on the careseeker and does not retreat into his or her own inner world. That is, the caregiver uses how and where the relationship with the careseeker touches the caregiver's self to further the careseeker's own self-exploration. This focuses the caregiver's attention on what it is like to be the subject rather than the target of the careseeker's wishes and demands.

This is all well and good as long as the careseeker evokes feelings, memories, and imaginings that do not provoke the caregiver's own anxiety, but as most caregivers realize, quite often careseekers do provoke anxiety. A prime reason people seek care is their inability to handle their own vulnerabilities. Caregivers must be able to put their own anxieties aside and tolerate their own feelings of vulnerability. Said another way, the caregiver must be able to tolerate feelings that are intolerable and unacceptable to the careseeker. In the language of ego psychology, this requires great ego strength.

Being able to put one's own anxieties aside means that caregivers must be well acquainted with their own sources of anxiety. One reason this is so important is the nature of anxiety itself. Anxiety cuts off foresight and undercuts objectivity. Anxiety obscures one's therapeutic judgment and diminishes ability to be empathic. Therefore, anxious caregivers are not very helpful to careseekers, since clarity of judgment and objectivity are two things careseekers cannot provide for themselves. It is these two things that the careseeker, one hopes, will integrate over time into his- or herself. This is not to say that a careseeker is totally lacking in objectivity or clarity, but that some anxiety blocks the careseeker from exercising what objectivity or clarity he or she has.

Another reason the caregiver's ability to put aside anxiety is important is that anxiety is unavoidable. The "sicker" the careseeker, the more easily and readily he or she will find the caregiver's vulnerabilities. It is beyond the scope of this book to dwell on this, but I will say that at a time when there is rampant sexual pathology, it is no wonder that caregivers find themselves having to carefully scrutinize their own sexual boundaries.

Anxieties bring caregivers' blind spots into view. To fully address the source(s) of anxiety, it is best if caregivers undergo their own therapy or are under some kind of collegial supervision.

Empathy is not what the caregiver guesses, intuits, or magically perceives going on in the mind of the careseeker. It is not being flooded by or taking over the feelings of another. Empathy is not being simply included in another's inner world, because empathy always includes a degree of objectivity; that is, an "outside" perspective. Empathy is the operation that defines the therapeutic field of inquiry. Empathy is a value-neutral tool of observation. Because empathy is a tool, it can lead to correct or incorrect results, be used with a variety of attitudes, and operate either rapidly and outside awareness or slowly and deliberately, with focused conscious attention. Empathy is a learned process that must be effectively used by a caregiver to be any good to careseekers at all. In addition, the more empathic the caregiver is, the more curative care will be.

Empathy is one person's attempt to experience the inner life of another while simultaneously retaining the stance of an objective observer.

Cognitive Processes in Empathy

Empathy, whether it operates inside or outside of awareness, involves the mediation of cognitive processes. Cognitive processes are essential to empathy. That is why an appropriate empathic response by a caregiver as a selfobject can be followed by an interpretation of the careseeker's inner world as it is currently understood by the caregiver. Empathic response enables the careseeker to feel understood by the caregiver. The role of the caregiver is to describe the careseeker's inner state to the careseeker. Empathic response demonstrates to the careseeker that the caregiver understands and to some extent experiences what the careseeker is experiencing, for example, joy, emptiness, or enhanced self-esteem. Empathic response signals to the careseeker that he or she has touched or connected with the caregiver, that the careseeker is not alone in feeling. Once the careseeker feels understood, and this may take many therapeutic hours, the caregiver can offer an interpretation or explanation.

Tony felt frustrated in his dead-end job. The counselor listened to Tony's description of his empty feelings. During the initial phase of caregiving, all Tony seemed to want from the caregiver was a silent presence. As the caregiver struggled to understand Tony, she often encountered Tony's shame and anger. But as she listened, she began to realize that although anger and shame were uncomfortable feelings for Tony, they were better than having no feelings at all. That is, experiencing anger and shame at least made him feel alive. The caregiver kept this hunch to herself for several sessions. Then Tony began a session with a harangue concerning a coworker. After twenty minutes of being angry and repeating the incident over and over, Tony finally said, "I'm repeating myself, aren't I?" The caregiver replied, "You seem reluctant to let your anger go." Tony's face reddened, but then he related a similar incident that had happened with his father when he was a boy.

Remembering that Tony's red face usually signaled both anger and shame, the caregiver later said, "Your red face usually means you are feeling both anger and shame. We've talked a lot about anger today, I'm just wondering if you are feeling shame too?" "You read me so well that it's scary," Tony smiled. "My father always thought he knew what was going on with me. He never did, of course. You seem to, though."

At this point the caregiver had a choice between saying, "Tell me more about your father" and "It's scary that I do?" The first response might uncover some memories associated with longings to feel understood by the father. The second would keep the focus on what is happening now between the caregiver and Tony. The caregiver opted for the second, hoping that Tony would talk about how he was experiencing her empathy. Tony continued, "It's scary to think that someone is paying so much attention to me. You listen to not only what I say, but you read between the lines too. My father never could, but hey, what could I expect, he was always working. Of course, he said that he worked so we kids could have it better than he did growing up. That's where the shame fits in. I felt ashamed that I didn't do more to help. I guess I still do. It's just when you see something I don't, it makes me feel that same old way. I know you are helping me, but I still believe that I should do more."

Tony went on to say that he always felt he had to do more, but he now felt all "used up." Feeling that he could not do what he thought he ought to do—more—stirred up intolerable feelings of dependence. His feelings were exacerbated by the reality that he had gone as far as he could in his job. Other employees had been promoted over him. He was no longer in his thirties or forties, on the way to the "top." He was in his fifties and in his mind lucky not to be laid off. For Tony, being in a dead-end job meant many things, but it especially meant he was increasingly dependent on the unreliable "good graces" of his firm.

In his counseling, Tony was feeling dependent on his caregiver. These feelings brought forth his ambivalence, particularly in regard to memories of his father. In Tony's inner world the choice was either be totally self-reliant and feel proud or be totally reliant on others and feel angry and ashamed. Being understood by the caregiver made Tony feel dependent. Said another way, being understood elicited a conflict in Tony, and this conflict highlighted the empathy he experienced and did not experience in his relationship with his father.

Said in the language of self psychology, when the counselor wondered aloud if Tony was feeling shame, Tony acknowledged that feeling, but something else happened too. Tony immediately spoke of a memory of his father who also "knew him well." Tony shifted away from his immediate relationship with the counselor and momentarily distanced himself from her, using the memory of his father. Counselor and father were associated in that instant not by what was said, or even perhaps how the words were said, but by what was felt: a longing to be fully understood but feeling disappointment and fear instead.

The counselor's attempt at empathy evoked Tony's feelings of fear and disappointment because Tony felt only partially understood by the counselor. The counselor's empathy was not quite good enough. It was just off the mark, because Tony experienced feeling understood as also feeling threatened. But it was a small empathic failure as opposed to a traumatic empathic failure on the part of the counselor. When Tony experienced this empathic failure by the counselor, he shifted the interpersonal focus to a past relationship with his father in which he felt the same way; namely, partially understood and fearful.

Tony turned away from the counselor's attempt at empathy to a memory of his father in an attempt to shore up himself and stop the fearful feelings. Tony was looking for solace and comfort in his past relationship with his father. He used his relationship with his father as a selfobject. Then Tony did something interesting. He compared the selfobject of his father with the counselor. Tony found that his attempt to dispel his fear by evoking the selfobject relation with his father also carried the message that Tony, himself, should have done more in the past and should be doing more now with the counselor, but he could not because he felt "all used up." The counselor then refocused Tony on his fear of feeling understood in the present by her in order to focus Tony on his conflict and invite him to struggle to find new ways to deal with his fear within the context of their relationship.

Tony turned to the selfobject relation of his father, but he did not back away from his counselor. He used his past relationship with his father in order to enter into a deeper relationship with the counselor. But then feeling closer brought forth his ambivalence toward feeling dependent and particularly feeling dependent on his father.

When the client feels understood, the caregiver may offer an explanation or interpretation. In the above example the explanation was the statement "You seem to be feeling shame." Interpretation is crucial because it enables an empathic bond with the careseeker that is based on a more mature relationship. That is, when the caregiver offers explanations, the caregiver retains objectivity. Over time this objectivity experienced in the relationship between the caregiver and careseeker is internalized within the careseeker, who more objectively understands him- or herself.

Learning to Be More Empathic

If empathy is the tool of caregivers, how can we learn to use it more effectively? Empathy consists of at least four distinct and probably sequential processes.

Resonance with the Feeling States of Another Person

One afternoon I met with a young man who was struggling to make an important decision. As he talked, my stomach felt as though it was "going wild." My immediate thought was of my lunch an hour earlier, and I decided I would not eat at that restaurant again. As the young man continued, I did my best to focus on what he was saying. Finally he stopped and blurted out, "I am in such inner turmoil." I thought, "You really must be." His inner turmoil was affecting my stomach. After he said this, he began to calm down, and my stomach relaxed as well. This is an example of what I mean by resonance.

Resonance is an act of resounding. Resonance, as I mean it, is a term borrowed from music. Resonance is also a term used in physics for a vibration of large amplitude resulting on application of a forced vibration to a system, when the period of the force equals that of a natural vibration of the system. The result is an intensification of tone. As I am using resonance, it implies an intensification of perception. In the fullest experience of resonance what resonates are the very structures of a person's inner reality.

Recently I read an article about opera singers who control the pitch, quality, inflection, and color of sound by the placement of maximum resonance. Low notes resonate in the chest, middle register notes in the mouth, and high notes in the cavities in the head. An acclaimed voice teacher once said that if we were sensitive enough, we would feel the vibration in our bones, which are hollow. Singers resonate with sound, and as they do so that sound is intensified. Through empathy, perceptions are intensified such that they are not as easily denied awareness.

Perhaps another example of resonance in its fullest sense would be helpful. This is a personal example that still evokes meaning despite its occurrence over twenty years ago. My family and I attended my sister's last orchestral performance as the first-chair cellist of her university. Soon she would embark on her graduate studies. The program was not particularly remarkable except that the last piece was a Beethoven symphony. There I was, sitting in Clowes Hall Auditorium where I had sat countless times before. I had attended concerts there even as a child and even remembered when the hall first opened.

As a child, I had dreamed that one day I too would play upon that stage. That dream had come true in a limited way, but here was my sister, my little sister, sitting at the head of her section playing the difficult runs of the Beethoven masterfully, easily. Her ease, grace, and even her cavalier manner were so typical of her. To her it was just another performance, but to me it was so much more. I felt the deepest core of my being resonate. I too had played that symphony. The feelings that welled up within me were so deep that I thought my heart would burst. Pride, envy, joy, sorrow, love, resentment all brewed within me. I wanted to keep this experience forever. As part of the audience I could feel immersed in her performance without experiencing the anxiety I usually felt when I performed. Those difficult and exposed violin passages caused me no end of anxiety.

No words can adequately describe what I experienced, but I know that seeing my sister play meant more to me than I could ever express. I felt beyond good or bad, beyond caring whether or not I cried; I felt deeply, clearly, meaningfully. And as I later learned, so did my parents.

Not all experiences of resonance are so vivid or dramatic. But when a caregiver listens to a careseeker, part of entering into the other's inner world is being with the other such that one is affected. The caregiver can resonate as long as he or she has no anxiety over being with the other, or can at least put that anxiety aside. An analogy might be helpful. The careseeker is like a tuning fork sending forth vibrations. The caregiver is like another tuning fork that begins to vibrate as a response. Anxiety in the caregiver acts as a damper and impairs the response.

I have asked other caregivers how they are affected by being with careseekers. Very often these caregivers respond in a visceral way to particular persons. One of my colleagues was so adept at this that the hospital emergency room staff would call him if they thought they were dealing with a schizophrenic. My colleague said he would perceive discomfort in his stomach if the patient was indeed schizophrenic. He thought of this affectation as an "empty hook."

One afternoon I was sitting with a woman who spoke in even tones and smiled throughout the session. As she talked, I began to feel my heart beat faster and then irregularly. This is not typical for me. I knew I was resonating with her. Because I recognized my sensations from similar experiences, I asked her if she was feeling angry. Her entire demeanor changed and she began to explain that she felt like her blood was "boiling."

Resonance involves paying attention to what I, the caregiver, perceive as I sit with a careseeker—not only what I see or hear the careseeker doing but how I am being affected in my own inner world, and how being with this particular careseeker impacts me in a concrete way.

I do not mean to suggest that the caregiver perceives only feelings. Often as a caregiver listens, memories, images, or fantasies also come into consciousness. As Tony talked about life with his angry father, the caregiver began to fantasize Tony's father pushing Tony over a cliff. The image of his own angry father began to take shape in the mind of the caregiver. Resonance is resounding with the inner world of the careseeker. It is a process by which the careseeker and caregiver connect in both conscious and unconscious ways.

Abstraction of Interpersonal Experience

The second process in empathy is abstraction of empathic knowledge from the interpersonal experience of emotional resonance. This is, simply put, describing with language the experience of resonance. Sometimes finding words to adequately describe resonance is difficult. The act of describing with language what one perceives is in some ways analogous to translating from one language into another. Some things just do not translate.

For instance, there are always words, phrases, and ideas in a given language that have no direct correlation in another language. The Hebrew interjection that is translated as "Behold!" in English connotes immediacy and an element of surprise. What is "beheld" is an undeniable reality. In Genesis 28:15 God says to Jacob, "Behold, I am with you." This statement means more than, "Look, see," or as the New Revised Standard version says, "Know that I am with you." It suggests God getting right up in Jacob's face and looking him squarely in the eyes. It suggests God jolting Jacob's reality with the fact of God's undeniable presence.

Attempting to describe one's experience of resonance is an act of abstraction. From the experience particular aspects are lifted out or given weight. This is not the same as reinforcing resonance, although putting perceptions into language may also have that effect. Putting the resonance into language also helps to formulate the experience of resonance by giving it added meaning. For example, Juan felt sad. As his caregiver resonated with Juan's feelings, the caregiver began to perceive something else mixed with the sadness. To the caregiver it felt like fear. The caregiver abstracted not only sadness but another emotion. When appropriate, the caregiver observed to Juan that his sad memories also contained fear. As Juan reflected on the caregiver's statement, he began to focus on his fear, thus expanding not only his inner awareness, but the meaning of his sadness.

These weighted aspects are meant to typify the whole. For example, if as I listen to a careseeker my heart begins to beat faster, I may describe this as racing or running away. Often I am not sure how to label my response until the careseeker says a word that seems to match.

Integration of Abstracted Knowledge

The third process in empathy is integrating the knowledge gained from resonance. The careseeker begins to think about what the empathic response means; that is, what can I infer?

As I have learned to "listen" to my body, I find that particular self-perceptions seem to correspond to particular feelings in the careseeker. Thus, a "racing" heart tends to mean that the careseeker is expressing fear. For me, a "pounding" heart tends to mean the careseeker is expressing anger. For my colleague, the "empty hook" tends to mean the careseeker is expressing intense ambivalence. The more I am aware of my own inner world, the more I can trust my empathy. This also means the more I can objectify my empathy the more I can use it as a methodological tool. Not all caregivers are equally sensitive to their bodies. Your experiences of empathy may affect you quite differently, but each caregiver brings out from his or her experience some way to use the empathy he or she does have to benefit the careseeker. A friend once told me that while he did not have much empathic ability to sense when things were going "right," he did have a great sensitivity to knowing when things were going "wrong."

If the caregiver is comfortable and confident using a particular theoretical approach, integration will also involve forming hunches about what empathic response means. These may not yet be well-formed hypotheses, but they are certainly more than intuition.

As the caregiver listened to Tony, he fantasized Tony's father pushing Tony over a cliff. The caregiver then began to perceive feelings of fear. Tony looked and sounded angry, but the caregiver was resonating with what seemed to indicate Tony's fear. At an appropriate place, the caregiver observed to Tony, "You are speaking with an angry voice, but there seems to be another feeling too." Tony responded, "My God, I'm afraid that I'm turning into my father." "Stay with the fear." "I'm not sure I can." "Try." "I'm so afraid that, well . . . I . . . might die." As counseling progressed, Tony learned how ashamed he was of his fear. The more Tony explored what anger, fear, shame, and hurt meant for him, the less depressed he felt.

Transient Role Identification

In the fourth process in empathy, transient role identification, the caregiver imagines what it must be for the careseeker to be a self given the particular interpersonal context. Ophelia grew up in a home where she felt little love. Her mother seemed to favor her brother. Her father was either emotionally distant or physically punitive. As a young child Ophelia concocted a fantasy that she was adopted. Surely these could not be her real parents. But she began to believe this fantasy was reality. Living with this fantasy was a way Ophelia shielded herself from feelings of rejection and abandonment. A caregiver had told Ophelia her fantasy was a lie. Ophelia took this to mean all fantasies were lies; lying was bad; therefore, she was bad. Ophelia felt emotionally distanced from and punished by that caregiver. While this experience felt oddly familiar, she also felt angry, so angry she quit counseling. Several months later Ophelia got up enough courage to call another caregiver. Ophelia related what had happened. While this caregiver had a hunch that Ophelia had helped set up the previous caregiver for failure, he nevertheless withheld this interpretation.

As the counseling progressed, the caregiver was able to imagine what it must have been like to be a little girl in Ophelia's household. As he did this, his capacity for empathy deepened, and paradoxically, so did Ophelia's need to set him up for failure. She needed him to both understand her and not understand her. This ambivalence is what the caregiver called to Ophelia's awareness again and again.

At the same time, the caregiver tried to imagine what it must be like for Ophelia to reveal herself to him in the therapeutic relationship. At one point he said, "I imagine that it must be difficult for you to be here with me sometimes." To this she replied, "I feel so unworthy."

Many sessions later Ophelia returned to this last observation by her caregiver. Not only had she felt accepted and affirmed as a self, but she heard something else. The words that made such an impression on Ophelia were "I imagine. . . ." In these words, Ophelia heard affirmation of her own imagination and fantasies. This affirmation freed Ophelia enough to see that reality did not have to be so fearful; thus, she strengthened her desire to live in the real world and was able to begin to accept the reality of her painful past.

Empathy involves the mediation of cognitive processes. Empathy is not just a cognitive process; it involves a sensitivity to self and other in relation, including a disciplined understanding of unconscious wishes and feelings. The goal of empathy in this context is to enable the careseeker to feel understood by the caregiver and then to integrate what being understood means here and now. This second step, integration, comes about through interpretation.

When the careseeker feels understood, the caregiver may offer an explanation or interpretation. Interpretation is crucial because it uses the empathic bond to move the careseeker toward greater self-objectivity. What happens is that over time the caregiver in the therapeutic role becomes a selfobject capable of soothing the self in times of anxiety. This soothing often entails containing feelings that had been unmanageable. If the caregiver's empathy proves "good enough," it will become a vehicle for enabling the careseeker to move toward richer and more satisfying relationships with self, others, and God.

Age-Appropriate Empathy

According to Kohut, empathy is limited to what is cognitively available to the person. Empathy is limited to what can be verbalized by a self in relation to another. This means that one cannot empathize with an infant or any other person who does not have a sense of self that he or she can verbally apprehend. A careseeker such as the one mentioned earlier who could only tolerate "uh-huh" from the caregiver may have a fragile sense of self, and empathy toward that self is very limited. A person such as this is not resisting the caregiver but entering into an interpersonal relationship as best he or she can. The depth and scope of the relationship is very limited because that is all the self there is to offer.

There is, however, a problem with Kohut's description of empathy. A person develops a sense of self and has selfobject needs long before verbal skills and cognitive apparatus develop. The infant has selfobject needs from the beginning. But how can an infant experience the empathic environment as empathic?

Kohut begins his developmental scheme with the young child between the ages of eighteen and twenty-four months. Prior to this for Kohut, the child exists as a virtual self; that is, the infant as an individual exists as a conceptualization of the parents and family. The child comes into a dynamic system of roles, beliefs, values, and expectations. Between the ages of eighteen and twenty-four months children demonstrate that they are beginning to organize individual experiences in terms of general categories of their own making. The key word in the previous sentence is "demonstrate," by which we mean young children begin to manifest the use of their own categories by verbal language. At about this age, a new organizing subjective perspective emerges and opens a new domain of relatedness, and that perspective is verbal language. The child begins a narrative of his or her own life from interpersonal experiences of meaning. This narrative was unknown before and cannot exist without words. But if we mean that before the age of eighteen to twenty-four months, the young child does not or cannot organize individual experience in terms of his/her own general categories, we are wrong. Early infant research suggests that infants have some organizing capabilities of individual experience in terms of their own general categories from birth.

Emergence of a Sense of Self and Selfobjects

Early infant research confirms that some sense of self exists in the infant, and that that sense of self exists prior to Kohut's beginning point of from eighteen to twenty-four months. Early infant research is important to caregivers because it helps us understand the process by and through which persons' sense of self and other emerges, including the divine Other. Given a set of developmental variables, science cannot predict with much accuracy what a particular person's sense of self and other will be, but science can offer us a way of understanding how the person got to where she or he is now and in some respects where she or he needs to go—that is, how she or he needs to be nourished on holy ground.

How does a person come to have a particular sense of self? This is not a new question. Since the Enlightenment it has been asked and answered numerous ways. But no matter how the question became an object of concern and for some a matter of ultimate concern, one thing is clear: being a self and having a sense of self is an important and often assumed part of life. Being a self and having a sense of it is considered a norm for human beings. Only when the self is called into doubt or thrown into crisis do people typically seek out caregivers, who help, in some sense, to find who and where they are, and sometimes who and where God is.

At the beginning of his developmental scheme Kohut presents us with a child capable of verbalizing and communicating shared interpersonal experience. He also presents us with a very young child (eighteen to twenty-four months) whose use of selfobjects appears full-blown. According to Kohut's description of development, an interpersonal relationship becomes the source of a selfobject because of empathic response. From the empathic responses, the child represents that person in the environment who is the source of empathy. This representation is called upon to play a vital role in sustaining or enhancing a sense of well-being and focus of the child's self. The selfobject shores up the self in times of distress. But how does an infant, who does not have the capacity for empathy, who indeed does not have the cognitive organizational skills for recognizing empathy, select, let alone represent, a person capable of empathic response? And if there are selfobject needs from the beginning as Kohut suggests, what or who can satisfy these needs if the infant is incapable of intrapsychic representation?

How selfobjects come into being and how their use emerges is not clear in Kohut's writing. Despite greater conceptual clarity in his last book, *How Does Analysis Cure?* on the subject of selfobjects generally, these questions are not fully answered. Kohut does hint that there are immature and mature uses of selfobjects as well as adaptive and pathological uses, but his primary focus is on the adult psychoanalytic patient.

In fairness to Kohut, one cannot expect his theory to exceed its limits. Empathy, his key methodological tool, cannot explore preverbalizable data. But within the scope of his method we can talk about possible preconditions that may "set the stage" for empathy. These preconditions might also help us understand how selfobjects are initially represented not only in the infant but in careseekers as well. If we explore how interpersonal experiences are construed as selfobjects in the preverbal infant, we may come to a clearer understanding of what constitutes nonlinguistic yet phase-appropriate selfobject response. This, in turn, may broaden the scope of caregiving to persons who have limited cognitive or verbal skills, such as mentally retarded persons and psychotic individuals. Further, if we have a clear understanding of how selfobjects emerge from interpersonal experience, we may find a clue to how a person can use a representation of God as a selfobject; that is, as a means of holding the self together in times of great anxiety.

The Importance of the Observed Infant

It seems obvious to me that no one can theorize about the infant's subjective experience of interpersonal relations without some kind of scientific data base which includes the observed infant. Before we start talking about the interpersonal life of the infant, we should know what one looks like. Before we scrutinize the meaning of adult memories of childhood recalled in the therapeutic relationship, we should have an understanding of how a child experiences reality. My own experience as a mother leads me to the conclusion that even knowing what an infant looks like is experience-distant, to borrow Kohut's phraseology, when compared to the experience-near stance of taking care of and loving a child.

It was not very long ago, according to my grandmother, that infants were left in their cradles for long periods, because people assumed babies could not "do" much else. Attitudes and various confidences in the capabilities of infants have even changed since I had my first baby fifteen years ago. Just think of the change of people's attitude toward nursing infants and the increased opportunities for involvement of the fathers in the delivery room, or, as it is often called now, the birthing room.

According to a recent study, we know that infants hear prenatally and can recognize the mother's voice at birth. A newborn can distinguish his or her own mother's milk from that of other mothers. Newborns prefer to look at human faces. At the age of two to three days, infants can discriminate and imitate smiles, frowns, and surprised expressions seen on a person's face. By five to seven months, infants can remember for more than a week a picture of a particular face that has been seen only once and for less than a minute. Thus long-term recognition memory functions, long before it was previously thought. This suggests that if long-term recognition memory functions, there must be some kind of intrapsychic representation.

All this early infant research suggests that infants have many more and more complex capabilities than previously thought. Current research suggests that infants are also far more individualistic than previously thought. But, of course, parents have always known that no matter how much two babies look alike, each is his or her own person from birth. One baby prefers to be rocked upright; one baby prefers being rocked cradled horizontally in mother's arms. Parents also know that babies make their preferences quickly and often loudly known.

Significance of Early Infant Research

Early infant research is of immense value to caregivers for understanding or interpreting the childhood beginnings of a particular conflict or problem, as often happens when dealing with sexual abuse or other childhood trauma. One key contribution of early infant research is the suggestion that the infant intentionally orders his or her interpersonal world from the beginning. This means that infants discover relationships and perceive reality through relationships. Said differently, children find themselves or come to themselves in relationships with significant others.

Another contribution is that the norm for ordering experience begins in infancy, perhaps prenatally. Infants cannot know what they do not know or that they do not know. This suggests that there are layers of memories or actual interpersonal experiences and that there are types of representations that exist beyond the limits of empathy. These layers of experience and representations might impinge on, circumscribe, or enhance a person's capabilities for empathy and recognizing empathic responses.

Another extremely important implication this infant research has for caregivers is that because the layers of experience and preverbal representations are not typically chaotic, that which is beyond the limits of empathy might not necessarily be chaotic either. Going to the limits of empathy is not necessarily like falling off the edge of the world. There is more beyond the horizon. Perhaps there is more hope for persons with psychosis and borderline states than theorists such as Kohut thought, because what is beyond the limits of empathy is not necessarily prepsychological.

What does all of this have to do with holy ground? When we accompany someone on holy ground our very presence there with the careseeker changes it. If we prove to have good-enough empathy, our relationship with the careseeker will change the way this reality is ordered, experienced, and thus recalled. Being nourished on holy ground means enhancing the careseeker's insight into his or her capabilities for empathy. It means being increasingly sensitive to how persons pattern interpersonal awareness.

Constructive Nature of the Interpersonal World

Early infant research supports the notion that infants seek out, participate in, maintain, and can avoid interpersonal relationship with particular people from birth. By age two to three months, infants seem to have an integrated sense of self. "Sense" means only non–self-reflexive awareness. This means simple awareness; that is, a direct experience, not concept, of reality. The words "of self" mean an invariant patterning of awareness, a form of organization. Infants are biologically programmed to initiate invariant patterning. This invariant patterning of awareness is the organizing of subjective experiences that will later be verbally referenced as the self. That is, the self is the organizing center of experience. This organization of subjective experience is the preverbal, existential counterpart of the objectifiable, self-reflective verbalizable self that is capable of empathy toward the self through the use of self-objects.

But what is patterned invariantly? Stern postulates that infants take sensations, perceptions, actions, cognitions, internal states of motivation, and states of consciousness and experience them directly in terms of intensity, shape, temporal pattern, vitality affect, categorical affect, and hedonic tone. These are the basic elements or categories of early subjective experience. Infants do not attend to specific domains of experience. All experiences become recast or patterned constellations of all the infant's basic subjective elements combined. In this way, the infant experiences reality as global. All incoming information is gradually and systemically ordered according to two kinds of invariants: self-invariants and other-invariants.

Basic Categories of Subjective Experience

Let us look at each of the basic categories of subjective experience in greater detail. *Intensity* has to do with the degree or amount of force. *Shape* refers to contour. *Temporal pattern* refers to amount, number, and rhythm. *Categorical affects* refer to the discrete states of happiness, sadness, fear, anger, disgust, surprise, interest, and even shame. They can appear alone or in combination. That is, one encounter with a single person can be both disgusting yet at the same time interesting. Often each categorical affect has a unique facial display. *Hedonic tone* refers to the pleasure and displeasure related to an experience. Stern introduces the term *vitality affect* to describe the dynamic, kinetic qualities: surging, fading away, fleeting, exploding, crescendoing, decrescendoing, collapsing, bursting, and drawing out. Vitality affects describe how an experience enters and leaves our field of attention. These qualities are elicited by changes in such things as motivational states and appetites.

Let us look at vitality affects in greater detail. The term *vitality* implies how affect endures or how an affect attracts someone's attention. An affect might appear all of a sudden (bursting), or slowly accelerate (crescendo) and disappear (explode). Although vitality affects are always associated with persons in the environment, vitality affects also seem to be related to bodily processes such as breathing, getting hungry, eliminating, going to sleep, and waking up. For example, going to sleep can be variously experienced as a slowing deceleration (decrescendo) or all of a sudden (collapse). Waking up can be experienced as a bursting forth or a gradual acceleration (crescendo). Death, which is often thought of as going to sleep, has been described as a fading away and birth as a bursting forth.

As mentioned earlier, Tony's red face signaled both shame and anger to his caregiver. From Tony's viewpoint, his shame and anger "burst" upon him. Often he did not realize his face was red until the caregiver observed it for him. Only then did Tony's awareness expand so that he felt his face get hot. Interestingly enough, the red face signaled to others his feelings while at the same time obscured his own awareness of his shame and anger. As Tony became better acquainted with his subjective experience of shame and anger, his face become red less often.

Often a careseeker will experience an amalgam of feelings during sessions. After talking about irrelevant topics for several sessions, one careseeker said he felt "blocked." He "knew" there was something he needed to get to, but he was having a difficult time doing so. He and his caregiver sat in a heavy silence for several minutes. He was having trouble staying focused on his feelings, but he continued to wade through what he termed confusion. The caregiver's association was a storm. At last he recalled a childhood memory. As he began to associate with what the memory evoked, huge waves of conflicting emotions emerged. The caregiver's image was of a great wad of feelings, tightly packed like a ball of aluminum foil. The caregiver asked him if he was aware of all he was feeling. He said yes. He felt hurt, anger, jealousy, disappointment, and fear all at the same time. The caregiver asked him to focus on the most predominant feeling. As he did so, he told a fearful tale of not being able to tell what was real and what was imaginary.

Global Nature of the Infant's Subjective World

According to Stern, infants are predesigned with the ability to transfer experience from one sensory modality to another. They are able to perform a cross-modal transfer of information that permits them to recognize a correspondence between what they touch and see, between what they hear and see, and so on. Infants seem to have amodal perception; that is, they are able to take information received in one sensory modality and translate it into another sensory modality. Even as adults, we retain some of this capacity. Experiments show we hear what we see being spoken. This means if one person watches another person speak, but cannot actually hear that person, the watcher nonetheless may literally *hear* something. The translation from one sensory mode to another is not simply a direct transfer across modalities; rather, it involves some kind of amodal representation that can be recognized in any of the sensory modes.

What happens to the global subjective world of the infant? Stern suggests that it remains the fundamental domain of human subjectivity, but that it operates out of awareness as the matrix from which thoughts, perceived forms, identifiable acts, and verbalized feelings will later arise. It becomes the matrix from which empathy is given and empathic response is received. Being empathic with a careseeker involves both an offering of one's self and a receiving of the other's self. This give and take in caregiving has been discussed using a wide range of metaphors, but I want to suggest that what is offered and received involves this matrix, which serves as a dynamic source of unconscious material.

I agree with Stern that this domain of human subjectivity is not a static artifact; it is a dynamic source of ongoing organization. While it operates out of awareness as a matrix, it can be indirectly experienced as a wellspring of creativity, and from it a person can experience a sense of coming into being. But I would go farther than Stern in saying that this matrix is not only a domain of human subjectivity but of intersubjectivity. This means that the self is always a self-in-relation, even at an unconscious level.

After months of counseling, Tony had a dream in which he was in a desert. This desert was a dark, foggy place and yet it also seemed to be in a valley or a hole. In the dream, Tony wanted to escape from the awful place, and suddenly he saw his caregiver above him with a rope in hand. The caregiver threw one end of the rope down, and Tony climbed out.

The associations connected with the dream involved the biblical story of Jacob. Jacob saw a ladder with angels ascending and descending to and from heaven. When Jacob awoke, he built an altar to the God of his vision and named the place Bethel. Tony associated his caregiver with the angels and the desert with his own life. As he talked about the desert of his dream he described it as a vast wasteland, actually more a marsh than a desert. The ground was solid yet sticky like mud. The whole place was dark, gray, and foggy. It was dark so he saw nothing, yet it was also gray, so he saw a little; it was foggy, so he groped his way along. As Tony explored this place in his mind, he began to feel more and more exposed in front of his caregiver.

As Tony talked, he began to shrink down in his chair. The caregiver leaned forward in her chair. Tony kept saying that he wished he could name the place. It was a place where he knew God needed to be and he said he was trying to let "him" in, yet he could not because of the fog. When the caregiver asked him where she was, Tony replied that she was there somehow, helping him find the door so God could come in. That the caregiver seemed to be inside scared yet comforted him. But he was very glad for the session to be over so he could climb up the rope and get out. This session was a turning point for the counseling relationship. As he discussed this session in subsequent visits, what was significant for him was the fact that the caregiver was in "there" with him. He discovered a representation of his caregiver in his inner world. Tony spent many sessions talking about both the scare and comfort he experienced.

Tony's dream is complex and can be conceptualized a number of ways. I want to point out that the longer Tony stayed with the images surrounding his dream, the less desolate they became. The desert went from being completely desolate to being a marsh, and the name he later gave it was a garden. The desert in the deep, dark hole became fertile ground. The caregiver's association with his naming the place a garden was the Garden of Eden, a holy place, where he felt free enough to feel affirmed and valued without shame.

Tony's garden became a place where he cultivated and ordered his interpersonal world. One outcome of his counseling was that he experienced a burst of creative energy.

I want to suggest that this example of Tony illustrates an adult experience of the global subjective world. This domain of Tony's inner world was accessible using images that were then organized into verbalized feelings. Once Tony could open this domain of himself up to an interpersonal relationship with his caregiver, he experienced increased creativity that took the form of a greater capacity for interpersonal intimacy. In a very real way, Tony's sense of self was enhanced. He experienced not only increased self-esteem but new aspects of himself that were now objectifiable, self-reflective, and verbalizable. His capacity for empathy and his recognition of the caregiver's empathy increased. Said another way, both he and his caregiver found themselves together on holy ground more often.

Early Representations

Infants are predesigned with an ability to transfer perceptual experience from one sensory modality to another. They seem to be able to take incoming information that is received in one sensory modality and translate it into another sensory modality using some form of amodal representation, a type of long-term memory that seemingly operates from birth. These early representations seem to reflect the world experienced as a perceptual unity. The infant's experience is global, yet he or she can abstract qualities from the environment such as vitality affects, and so on, and organize them according to self- and other-invariants. From these early representations, which include self-regulating others, mentioned in the first chapter, the infant gradually develops an increasingly organized sense of self.

Psychologist, I. H. Paul says that a person experiences the pattern of relating rather than particular experiences. Particular experiences are integrated into the preexisting patterns, which include a patterned representation of the self, other, self-with-other, and other-with-self. As experiences are integrated into the ongoing sense of self (and other), they are compared, weighed, and even perceived according to preexisting patterns. If, for example, someone frightens me, I perceive this experience as part of a pattern called fear and a pattern of relating to that person and others who frightened me. I then will recall this particular experience from within a context of similar experiences.

There is a dynamic relation between the particular experiences and the general patterns, for as the particular is evaluated by general preexisting patterns, so the particular can alter the overall pattern. Stern suggests with many other developmental authorities that infants pattern what they abstract from isolated events beginning from birth, if not before. Because the infant has amodal representation, he or she can approach a new encounter with a sense that it is not entirely new. In other words, new or novel does not necessarily mean foreign. For example, the infant recognizes the mother at birth due to prenatal familiarity with the varying patterns of her voice. Hearing the mother's voice, which is one sensory modality, can be translated across other sensory modalities such as smell, so that the infant can recognize the mother's milk. Hence when the infant begins to suck, which is a predesigned motor reflex, the infant roots toward a breast that is already in some sense familiar. Particular experiences with the breast as a particular object are integrated into the preexisting patterns of what will eventually be known as mother and self. Birth is not an introduction of the infant to the world, it is rather a new phase in that relationship. This fact is often reinforced by the mother's own feeling that she becomes a mother long before her child is born.

Episodes as Basic Units of Memory

A person integrates interpersonal relationships that include a relation with the self into episodes. An episode is made up of small elements or attributes. These attributes are sensations, perceptions, actions, thoughts, affects, and goals that occur in temporal, physical, and/or causal relation so that they are coherent. An episode occurs within one single, physical, motivational setting. Events are processed in time and causality is inferred, or at the very least expectations are set.

Consider these attributes: feeling happy, sitting in a chair, seeing the caregiver, smelling the caregiver's perfume, the caregiver begins to drum her fingers on the desk. We might call this episode "caregiver drumming her fingers." If this episode occurs more than once, the careseeker can recognize which features of the episode are similar and gradually with more episodes of this kind, the careseeker forms a generalized caregiver-drumming-her-fingers episode.

Every time this episode happens, there is a deviation from the generalized episode. Perhaps the caregiver frowns or the careseeker fidgets. The expected course of events has been altered. This new episode, "caregiver frowns," has violated the expectations of the generalized episode. The new episode is distinctive enough to be discriminated from the prototype. As a result of the discrimination a number of things can happen: (1) the single caregiver-frowns episode may never happen again, but may be remembered as a specific memory, (2) the caregiver-frowns episode may recur and form a new generalized memory, or (3) the new generalized memory may replace or alter the caregiver-drumming-her-fingers episode such that the careseeker may eventually expect a frown the moment the caregiver begins to drum her fingers.

A generalized episode is not a specific memory but is rather a structuring or patterning about the likely course of events and presumed expectation of actions, feelings, sensations, and so on. The presumed expectations may or may not occur. What is important is that interpersonal relationships are generalized or typified and represented *preverbally*, and then integrated into episodic memories. Stern calls these "representation of interactions that have been generalized" (RIGs). These RIGs will be of the utmost importance as we enter into a discussion of how persons relate to God.

RIGs

Representations of interactions that have been generalized, or RIGs, are a basic unit of the self. From various RIGs the self who acts, the self who feels, the self who is soothed—all the unique perceptions about the self—slowly coalesce. What will become complex and multidimensional representations of self begin as distinct representations based on specific RIGs. Gradually distinct representations are woven together into what Stern calls "islands of consistencies." Hence, for example, when the self needs soothing, that person's mind has a generalized representation of someone who soothes. To use a foreground and background metaphor, when the self who needs soothing is in the foreground, there is always a RIG of another in the background. Conversely, when the other is in the foreground, there is always a RIG of a self who needs soothing in the background.

Note that RIGs are subjective patterning of experience. A RIG is something that has never actually happened before and yet takes into account only things that have actually happened. It is a representation and not an activated memory.

What happens to a RIG when it is recalled into active memory? To answer this question, let's review. Episodes are the basic units of memory. Episodes are the patterning of attributes. Patterning implies organization in which some attributes predominate. The attributes of interpersonal experiences are patterned into representations of interactions that have been generalized, the RIGs. These RIGs are themselves the episodes of interpersonal relationships as experienced by the subject, the individual. Because RIGs are organized attributes, a RIG can be recalled by the reexperience of an attribute that is contained in the RIG. An attribute can be a sensation, perception, action, thought, affect, and/or goal that occurs in temporal, physical, and/or causal relation. The reexperience of an attribute allows it to be in the foreground of subjective experience and thus marked as relevant to the retrieval of a particular RIG.

For example, an infant is asleep in her crib at night. She is hungry, so she recalls the representation of her father who generally brings her a bottle. Still asleep, she begins to anticipate, so she begins to suck. When she is sufficiently hungry she wakes up crying from hunger, but also with rage. Her RIG includes her having a nice full feeling. She recalled the RIG of the father with her bottle, but there was no accompanying good feeling. So she cries. Her father appears, bottle in hand, and the nice full feeling returns as she takes the bottle. As the infant learns about being hungry, she will eventually expect father with her bottle to appear. The rage will diminish, and possibly the infant will stop crying when she hears her father's approaching steps, because she knows her bottle and her nice full feeling is coming. The attributes of being hungry in this particular way will always activate the RIGs of her father and of herself as hungry and satisfied. What is important here is that at this early stage of development RIGs are highly specific and are associated with specific events, and when RIGs are recalled, the infant gets a dose of the actual experience. That is, the infant actually experiences the presence of the self-regulating other, in this case the father who regulates both her hunger, nice full feeling, and rage. Said another way, the father-bringing-bottle experience contains that which is beyond the infant's ability to control without the father.

The Evoked Companion

When the generalized representation (RIG) is activated, the infant encounters an evoked companion. The RIG is a representation and not an activated memory. A RIG can be recalled, but once it enters activated memory, it involves an evoked companion. Let me carefully unpack this statement. In the above example, the father-bringing-bottle is that evoked companion. The evoked companion is an exemplar derived from a RIG that can enter into lived experience. RIGs are averaged experiences, but abstract representations that set up expectations for future events. Future events are judged and evaluated by the pattern of past events and not the past events per se. What is more important is that from the patterns of generalized representations an exemplar can appear. This exemplar has a more complex organizational status. An exemplar is not just a pattern of experience but a model of what should be and what ought to happen in particular circumstances. Hence it is derived from the abstract representation, but it is a concrete instance of that abstract representation.

As a concrete instance it is experienced, at least by the infant, as a real presence of someone who is a self-regulating other, that is, someone who can change and who has changed self-experience. Not only that, but an evoked companion is the presence of one who embodies in a very specific way how self-experience ought to change and what that change ought to be.

Evoked companions function to provide a constant interpersonal environment for the infant. Once cued memory has begun to function, infants are rarely alone. Infants encounter real external persons some of the time, and evoked companions almost all of the time. The concept of the evoked companion is related to the internalization of what is termed object constancy, but it is beyond the scope of this book to pursue this point.

Evoked companions are used throughout life, but at some point it is no longer necessary to recall the evoked companion to get a dose of the lived experience. An attribute alone may serve as a cue that can alter behavior, without a reliving of the generalized event. But relivings can and do often occur, especially when a person has been traumatized. The mechanics of these relivings are not clearly understood, but they are manifested in flashbacks and perhaps in nightmares associated with traumatic events. More commonly, adults do not necessarily need to feel the presence of an evoked companion, but only, for example, as the voice of his or her conscience.

Despite the fact that the evoked companion can be experienced as self-regulating, the integrity of the core sense of self and the core sense of other is never breached. For example, even one's own conscience is sometimes experienced as hearing a voice that is somehow not one's own. A four-year-old in our church told me that Jesus spoke to her. No, it was not like hearing the voice of her mother; it was a little voice inside her head that told her if something was good or bad. She rather liked this voice, because it helped her out a lot. "He" spoke to her as though he knew her. She, in turn, had learned about

Jesus in Sunday school. She knew that Jesus loved her, so she figured that it must be his voice she heard. She also had been taught that Jesus lives inside people, so she figured that he was a little man who lived in her head and whispered in her ear.

My daughter had a rather different experience. When she was about three to four years old, she too began having a conscience. As I was researching this area, I asked her about it. I had already had the encounter with the little girl mentioned above, and I wondered whose voice my daughter heard. While she knew Jesus loved her, she made it clear she did not want him living inside her. That scared her. She was a little girl; Jesus was a big man. She did not even want the picture book with Jesus' picture in her room at night. As far as she was concerned, the voice she heard telling her right from wrong was just some older version of her own. Interestingly enough, and perhaps not coincidentally, baby Jesus was a lot safer to her.

While the integrity of the core sense of self and the core sense of other are never breached, there is such a thing as a "we" experience. This is different from the experience of "I-with-another." The point is that when the infant recalls the soothing-other, the infant always recognizes that it is another who is causing the soothing. The effect is the soothed self. The infant may not fully understand how or why soothing is needed, but the infant knows who can soothe, the self-regulating other. The infant, as parents know, also has preferences of which self-regulating other is needed when.

Let us look at the theoretical implication closely. Again a foreground/background metaphor is helpful. According to this theory, from the infant's point of view, the world is not completely manageable; she or he needs a self-regulating other. The infant recalls a RIG that is capable of managing an episode. Note that this episode would include a RIG of a needful self in the foreground and a RIG of the self-regulating other in the background. The RIG of the needful self would include attributes of a self who is already soothed as a result of the impending interaction. Hence as the activated RIG, or evoked companion who soothes, moves into the foreground it must include some reference to the needful self and the soothed self as part of the background or else there can be no basis to discriminate between the expectations of being soothed and the activity that may or may not result in soothing.

While it may be helpful to maintain a theoretical distinction between the self who needs soothing, the other who soothes, and the self who is soothed as a result, in reality the situation is appreciably more complex. The self who needs soothing, the other who soothes, and the self who is soothed are RIGs, each of which contains attributes of the others. Not only that, but when one

RIG is in the foreground of experience, other RIGs or attributes of them are in the background.

But who is doing the soothing? The infant's self uses the self-regulating other. The infant may not be aware of the nature of his or her own agency in using the evoked companion, because it may operate outside of awareness. This would imply that some separation anxiety would involve the infant's growing recognition that the self-regulating other, the evoked companion, is *really* not there.

Models of Models: A New Experience of Abstraction

With the advent of verbalization at eighteen to twenty-four months, phase-appropriate empathic response takes on another dimension, consensual validation. This is where Kohut begins his developmental scheme. From ages two to four, Kohut says, the child looks to the parents for a recognition of the child's valued presence. The child searches for the gleam in the parent's eye. The child has been looking all along, but now the search has added meaning. The child has a new capacity that has emerged sufficiently to be used to organize interpersonal relations. Language makes abstract, objectifiable experience possible. Now the personal, immediate empathic response can be made impersonal and abstract.

The new capability gives selfobjects another dimension. Where before selfobjects were enmeshed in personal, immediate empathic response, they now can be objectified. But even objectified selfobjects, such as the "voice" of one's conscience, are never completely devoid of images, attunements, and regulatory aspects that were a part of their formulation.

Because language recasts all available memories and experiences, the evoked companion reflects this difference as well. But echoes of the evoked companion can be activated by an attribute of interpersonal experience with the represented person. For example, a little boy knows he has done the best he can when he hears his mother's affirming voice. He knows that his mother is "with" him when he gives all he has. If she typically shares and gives an empathic indication that she recognizes his efforts, the boy feels understood. "Encouragement" as an abstract idea might include this image of his mother. As the boy matures, he may evoke the image of his mother in order to reach for something he feels is beyond his grasp. The toy he reached for as a child might be replaced by the concept of success. But whether he consciously evokes the image of his mother or not, she will always be part of the background where encouragement is foregrounded.

Even infants are able to generalize experiences and abstract particular aspects of experience. They abstract, average, and represent information preverbally. What happens to representations of abstracted experience? As I have previously stated, evoked companions are models; that is, they are abstractions based on the patterning of experiences. But it seems logical that once language enters in, another level of abstraction is possible. Now there can be models of models. It would seem that some models can become prototypic for models in general. I propose that a person's representation of God can be an example of a model that becomes prototypic for other models. That is, God as an evoked companion can become the prototype of other evoked companions or selfobjects. A person's God can be an evoked companion par excellence. That person's representation of God can then become what Kohut calls a substitute selfobject; that is, a selfobject that can protect the personality from suffering permanent damage, especially during times of solitude. When there is no relationship upon which a person may draw, that person still has a means to soothe and defend the self. This selfobject can provide the person with great strength and courage to perform acts that could not otherwise be performed without the aid of a supportive group or despite extreme social disapproval.

However, God as the evoked companion par excellence can be a powerful obstacle in caregiving. For instance, when the caregiver fails the careseeker, even nontraumatically, the careseeker may turn to an image of God in an attempt to find satisfying soothing at the expense of the relationship with the caregiver, thereby continually restricting the depth and scope of the interpersonal relationship. In the mind of the careseeker, the caregiver's empathy may never be good enough. If this happens, the caregiver may be sure that the careseeker has been traumatized, and that there is immense anxiety about entering into interpersonal relationships generally. With such a person the caregiver must be kind, long-suffering, and patient. But the caregiver must also be prepared to not be good enough; that is, to have one's own narcissism assaulted.

Evoked Companion Par Excellence

Rizzuto says that, unlike other representations, a person's representation of God may gain a superior status over other representations. She says this is especially true during times of crisis or otherwise intolerable psychic pain. She further says that a person's representation of God may play an important role in maintaining psychic balance. But why? Why is the representation of God so central to the self?

There are many answers to this question. One is that God created us that way. God created humans with a need for God's self. Without going further into that, here I merely want to say that people's images of God can be as varied as spaceman, magician, Santa Claus, Baker Woman. Even the images of God in the Bible vary tremendously. There is the God who orders the murder of innocents, and there is the God who innocently died for sinners. There is the God who is a shield and fortress and the God who exposes, the God who loves and the same loving God who condemns.

Theologians grapple with the meaning of God for the church and the meaning of the church for God. But caregivers sit and listen to individuals' private renderings of those abstract meanings. I have often heard people, not just in counseling sessions but in church school, ask, "Who is God to me?" "Who is my God and how is my God related to the God of the church?" These questions are often asked when a person is in crisis or turmoil. Personal and profound, these questions impact not only the individual asking but the community of believers as well.

I cannot hope to answer these questions for careseekers. Often, as a caregiver, the best I can do is to listen to people's questions and wonder with them. I do know, however, that personal experiences with God are not rare, and that private and personal images of God are often called upon for solace and comfort when someone feels lost and alone. I am also aware that some images of God are neither soothing nor comforting, but in all cases the person's image of God says something profound about the core of the self.

Conclusion: Changing Images of God

Being nourished on holy ground often means that a careseeker's image of God changes. How does this happen? The careseeker gradually integrates the caregiver's empathy into the image of God. Or said another way, the caregiver's empathy frees the careseeker to receive God's love.

The concept of selfobject offers a helpful way to think about a person's representation of God. That representation can be used to effect self-repair, but the concept of the evoked companion related to the notion of selfobject adds another dimension. Stern's concept suggests a way that this one selfobject can gain a superior status over others, because it becomes a model of what all other models of soothing *ought* to be. It also gives a means to understand why a person's representation of God may be experienced as vividly real: because through it, one can subjectively experience what it ought to mean to be loved and cared for. The evoked companion embodies the worth and value of that person. God, as the evoked companion par excellence, embodies the ultimate worth and value of self and others. It can be experienced as a living presence. Further, because the evoked companion emanates from the core of the self as part of the self's matrix, it is central to the self's sense of its own well-being. Hence if someone experiences an image of God as problematic, there can be profound reverberations in the self's interpersonal relations, including the self's own attempts to soothe itself.

Tony felt shamed and angered by his dependency needs. Not surprisingly, his representation of God was of a God who valued independence and punished dependence. Hence, it was impossible for Tony to feel comfortable depending on others. Feeling the pain of shame and anger were preferable to feeling dependent; therefore, he projected his dependence on his wife, in particular, whom he then devalued. Feeling dependent on his caregiver was very difficult. He and his caregiver spent many months dealing with this issue in many forms, until Tony finally was able to accept that being dependent did not mean he was nothing. As he learned what "not being nothing" was, his image of God also changed. He was able to see God cry; that is, show compassion and mercy. God's tears of compassion nourished Tony and ushered him into greater self- and other-awareness. Being nourished on holy ground meant Tony found a deeper sense of who he was in relation to others.

～ 4 ～

Sharing the Fruit

STANDING ON HOLY ground, surveying holy ground, being nourished on holy ground—this is a way to describe the intimacy experienced and facilitated in a therapeutic relationship. But as previously mentioned, caregiving involves not only a holding environment but also sending forth. It is not only a process of self-understanding but a discovery of an enhanced sense of self-in-relation. The ultimate purpose of caregiving is to heal a careseeker so that he or she can empathically share the fruit of his or her discoveries with other selves-in-relation in the direction of greater depth and scope.

Previous chapters have given examples of people discovering, surveying, and being nourished on holy ground. But in this chapter, I will illustrate the entire process with one careseeker, and show how she came to share her fruit. This case is a composite drawn from cases of several actual careseekers. All pertinent personal information has been altered to protect confidentiality.

The Case of Joanne

Joanne was thirty-three, a white, married homemaker. After college she worked in a laboratory doing analytical work. After marriage she and her husband settled into a comfortable suburban life. She was an active church member and devoted mother. Although she saw herself as not having enough self-discipline, she said she was fairly happy with her life. Because most people initially come into counseling at a time of crisis, the noncrisislike nature of Joanne's presenting "problem" seemed curious to me, her caregiver. Joanne insisted, however, that she just wanted a place to "talk about herself." While she was concerned about being overweight, she thought this would "take care of itself." It took Joanne several months finally to determine why she had come to counseling, and it was many months before I found a satisfying answer to my question, "Why me, now?"

Counseling as Self-Caretaking

Joanne was a kind, outgoing person. She was about fifty pounds overweight, but attractive. She always came to counseling "dressed up." "Dressing up" was something she generally did on "special" occasions. Her appointments were on her "mother's day out" times. On these days, she treated and indulged herself by eating lunch at a restaurant with a friend, shopping, or otherwise being "out" in the world. Given the seeming lack of urgency, we set appointments once a week. Joanne saw counseling as taking care of herself. For her, it was a means toward self-improvement and a way to enjoy herself with only minimal guilt. This was the one day she laid aside the responsibilities of motherhood and homemaking. In some respects, her day out was her Sabbath, her day of refreshment and replenishment.

Joanne paid me out of her own earnings. She had turned a hobby into a small business and thought of this money as her own. This method of payment signified to her that therapy was her own, too. It made her feel self-sufficient and less dependent on her husband. In short, being able to pay for her own counseling was a way Joanne boosted her self-esteem. "Paying her own way" was how Joanne "owned" her counseling as real and important. Yet, by paying with "her" money, she began therapy thinking of it as a luxury, something that was not a necessity.

Looking back upon my decision to allow Joanne to pay me a fee based solely on her own earnings rather than the family earnings, my usual procedure, was probably a mistake. In this way, I colluded with her defenses and allowed her to avoid her anxiety. If anxiety is understood as the "motor" of therapy, allowing Joanne to avoid hers was almost like turning the motor off. In retrospect, this may have been one of the reasons it took Joanne so long really to commit to the counseling process and to connect with me. Joanne did not need my empathy because she could maintain a view of herself as self-sufficient and not dependent in a significant way.

Counseling History

Joanne took months to understand why she had sought a female pastoral caregiver for counseling. Previously, she had seen a male pastoral counselor, but only for a few sessions. Joanne said her previous counselor disappointed her, because he was fat and talked about himself too much. She said that he seemed to really enjoy their conversation, but increasingly she did not. She began asking herself, "Who is the counselor?" and "Who is getting counseled?"

She broke off this counseling relationship because she felt she was not "getting anywhere." While she denied feeling a need to really "go" anywhere with me, she intuited that not "getting anywhere" felt like going backward.

As Joanne spoke about her previous counselor, she said she felt frustrated. She was frustrated, because she felt robbed of her own special time for herself. He was being selfish and "hogging" her time. Further, he was fat. How could he talk about her lack of self-discipline when he apparently had none himself? But what frustrated her the most was that she felt she did all the giving in the counseling and was not getting anything back in return. While she tended to feel this in all her relationships, she recoiled at feeling it there with him.

The final blow came when he suggested that counseling was a way to get help for her weight problem. Now, to admit she needed counseling was a narcissistic injury anyway, but to define her problems for her was the last straw. Joanne had already decided that her major issues centered on a lack of self-esteem. She believed her weight was secondary. She thought that if counseling focused on self-esteem, the weight would take care of itself.

Emergence of Issues

Joanne felt out of control. Feelings of helplessness and anxiety manifested themselves in binge eating, problems in disciplining her children, and a vague dissatisfaction with her husband. She felt that when her children were "unruly," if she punished them "like they ought to be punished," they would reject her. Although she described herself as happily married with a satisfying sexual relationship with her husband, she also felt that intimacy with him was lacking something.

When Joanne looked at her life, it was "perfect." She had a "happy" home, happy children, and a successful husband. But if everything was so wonderful, why was she so depressed, she wondered. She had tried to express her feelings to a close friend, but Joanne seemingly could not communicate her feelings effectively. It was ironic, she thought. She was so outspoken, so intelligent, but could not really decide how she felt about herself. She did know that she was trying to eat her problems away, trying to fill some inner emptiness. If she could only see what her problems were, she thought, she would deal with them in a different way. Gaining weight only confirmed her low self-esteem as a failure.

After several sessions of telling me how wonderful her life was, she finally admitted that she was feeling very depressed. Depression was, for her, a hollow, empty feeling. Joanne's admonition confirmed a recurring fantasy I had as I sat with her. I imaged her as a piece of cake with lots of sticky icing that tasted stale. Another image was that all there was was icing with no cake inside.

As Joanne described herself, she said that her senses were dull. The world looked dim. She had an edge to her voice when she wanted to be heard. In short, her life lacked spontaneity and vitality. At first she thought that perhaps part of her depression was an expression of her guilt for thinking something was wrong with her or her family. She also realized that anger was there "somewhere," but her intuition was that this depression had very deep roots. While it was somewhat distressing, it also felt familiar. In fact, the more she thought about it, the more she began to think that she had not been without some form of it for a very long time.

Standing on Holy Ground

As Joanne talked, she also began to feel close to me. Feeling warmth toward me was not altogether comforting, because it seemed to indicate that she was missing something at home. This became especially clear during one session. Joanne had been talking about her distress concerning her children. At an appropriate place, I said that while I could see by her face that she felt sadness, she was not communicating that feeling to me. She sat speechless for a long two minutes, and then began to cry. She then talked about her tears as she expressed both anger and sadness. How could I possibly know what life was like for her? On one hand, she was glad I had no weight problem and that I was such a successful career woman, but on the other hand, she was jealous of my happiness, my competence, my "wonderful" family life. And yet, despite what she took to be our differences, she felt I really understood her. She felt I could empathize with her, and slowly she began to trust me.

When I said that she was not communicating her feelings to me, it "rang true" to her. And yes, it felt significantly different to her when she kept her feelings inside and when she let someone share them with her. When she shared her feelings with me, she was also open to receive my empathy. For the rest of the session, she reflected on what those differences meant to her. This was Joanne's first discovery on holy ground with me.

In psychological terms, from the beginning of counseling, Joanne sought to use me as an idealized selfobject. As an idealized selfobject I became an image of perfection with whom she could be a part. I became a refuge of serenity and power when she felt lost and out of control. Yet feeling safe with me was a narcissistic injury, because she was also feeling increasingly dependent on me. These feelings of dependence ran diametrically opposed to her desire to be self-sufficient. Hence, Joanne felt ambivalent toward me and toward counseling.

Joanne acted out her ambivalence in ways particular to her, but also in ways that most caregivers will recognize. While she did idealize me as successful, competent, a model wife and mother, a picture of health in my size-six suit, she was also adept at finding, and upon occasion creating, small personal flaws. For example, didn't working also mean that my children were deprived in some way? I had to work so many hours; therefore, my husband must not be very successful as opposed to hers. I would be so much more attractive if I changed the color of my hair. Joanne took great pleasure in setting me up on a pedestal and then tipping it so I would fall off. While she never really "pushed" me off the pedestal, she did try to find ways to make me slip off. Consequently, I became more adept at accepting the "slings and arrows" of narcissistic injury myself as I sat with her. In this way, she enabled me to be more empathic with her own hurts.

Joanne sought to raise her own self-esteem at the expense of that of others. Hence tipping the pedestal, or attacking my self-esteem, was an indication of her own neediness as well as of her ambivalence. If I was not so powerful, she would not need to feel dependent on me. Yet she also needed me to be "perfect" whatever that meant to her (and it changed over time) so that she could join me there.

In addition to raising her self-esteem at the expense of that of others, she did not have a set of clearly defined goals. She did not know where she wanted to go or what to do with her life. Her feelings of being out of control reflected, in part, her feelings of being lost and trapped within her "perfect" world. Being "found" by my empathy carried with it the anxiety of discovering that her world was not giving her what she thought it should. Hence she was frustrated, which meant disappointed and angry. The concomitant rage she kept smoldering under a layer of depression.

But these were not new issues, so why did she seek counseling now? Joanne's youngest son had just started kindergarten. He was excited about going to school in a big yellow bus, but Joanne was devastated. Her son had left her, and he seemingly felt no remorse. He did not miss her at all. In fact, he generally refused to tell her what he did at school, and he certainly did not want her to be "room mother." Joanne was wounded to the quick, and this narcissistic injury recalled a much deeper psychic pain.

Surveying Holy Ground

Surveying holy ground means looking at what is of value to the careseeker—not so much what the careseeker says is important, but what convictions stir deep emotions within the careseeker. Religion was important to Joanne, and she wanted it to be important to her caregiver as well. The high valuation of religion was part of the answer to "Why me, now?" She figured that was guaranteed if the caregiver worked as a church professional. A church professional, in her eyes, must be a serious and devoted Christian.

The Importance of Religion

Joanne talked a lot about her religion but very little about God. God, to her, was a forbidding and distant figure. Her religion was largely a set of rules and wise prescriptions for living. Her church offered her a place where she was important and upper-middle-class people with whom she could feel kinship. She expected her church to raise and support her self-esteem by rewarding her with positions of authority. Then she wondered why it was that she always seemed to end up in charge of this or that program. She supposed it was because she felt responsible for the well-being of her church and the successful performance of its duties. It was not until much later in counseling that she discovered how she communicated her wishes to be authoritative.

Childhood Memories of Father

Surveying holy ground with Joanne also meant putting her memories in perspective. Joanne remembered very little of her childhood. What memories she had were dominated by feelings of anxiety. She said that she was a good child as children go (a very "loaded" statement), but she could not possibly imagine what awful things her father thought she might do if he was not there to "hold the line."

The most vivid memory of her childhood centered on the last times she saw her father, who died when she was eight. Shortly before his unexpected death, Joanne and her brother were arguing. Joanne's father burst angrily into her room and told them to stop. Later that night, he went to the hospital. The next time Joanne saw him, he was "hooked up" to all sorts of tubes and machinery. If only she had known he was so sick, the child Joanne thought, she would have tried harder to be a good girl.

The trauma of seeing her father, the most powerful person she knew, helplessly attached to a life-support system shattered her idealized image of him. She had only known him as self-sufficient and independent. Joanne was also very afraid of this powerful man. He shouldered larger-than-life responsibilities, and he was a devoted Christian, but he evoked great fear in his children. Not until the end of counseling could Joanne remember a time when she had ever felt warm about and close to her father. And her father had left her despite the prayers of the church people, the prayers of her mother, and Joanne's own pleas.

Joanne secretly believed that her father died for some sin she had committed. He was such a good man that surely it was not he who was being punished. After all, she was the one who started the argument with her brother, if not that time, sometimes. The idea that the "wages of sin are death" was not her idea, but her father's and the church's, so it must be right. Yet, although one idealized image of her father was shattered, another took its place: the idealized image of the suffering parent who sacrifices self for "his" children.

Much of the anger that she felt toward her father for leaving her was displaced onto God. Although God was very big and powerful, he was also dangerous. It was best not to be angry with God. God might punish her, or, worse, demand her life, too. Joanne repressed her anger and pushed God away.

But Joanne could not so easily repress her fears of abandonment. The loss of her father was so painful that she had found a way for him still to be with her. Interestingly enough, Joanne remembered the time and place this probably happened. Joanne's brother cried as the family gathered around the father's deathbed, but Joanne did not feel sad. She was fascinated by the medical machinery. The wires and tubes seemed "clean" and "uncomplicated." The shattering of an idealized image of a strong, responsible parent was transformed into an idealization of science. Her idealized selfobjects, including her idealized image of her father, became associated with scientific mechanisms.

As eight-year-old Joanne watched her father die, she idealized that which contained the possibility of saving her father's life, Science. God might not save him, but Science, if properly applied, could. Joanne's faith in her childhood God was diminished and replaced, to some degree, by her faith in Science. Her fantasy connected with this hospital scene was that if the equipment had been better, her father would have lived. She could have saved her father, if she had known more. Henceforth, she had a responsibility to learn all she could about Science. Taking on responsibility was something that would make her father proud, so she obeyed and burdened herself for life with self-inflicted blame.

Being responsible also made her feel closer to her father, because through shouldering responsibilities she became like him. But as she grew older, she found being like her father also had painful consequences. She put so much value on taking responsibilities that she had a difficult time accepting help when those responsibilities weighed too heavily on her.

As child development experts inform us and as we as caregivers and parents know, at about age eight or nine children typically deal with certain moral dilemmas. These dilemmas generally center on ideas of fairness and responsibility. Children at this age have a clear understanding of what rules are and what the consequences are if rules are broken. In Joanne's eight-year-old mind her father had obeyed all the right rules, but he was punished. This meant to her that someone else must have broken one of God's rules. In a gesture of some grandiosity, she named herself. While this comforted her in so far as she "made sense" of what was otherwise an insoluble moral dilemma, it nevertheless did not seem fair. The lack of fairness on God's part was frustrating to Joanne, because not only was God not right to be unfair, but God now also seemed capricious, that is, not completely in control, not worthy of her dependence when she felt out of control. Thus, in a convoluted way, Joanne used God to shore up her defensive self-sufficiency.

While many children lose a parent through death, still more lose parents through divorce. To a younger child, up to about age four, loss through divorce and death can feel about the same. In some cases of divorce, however, there is the added dimension in that the child may have great anger over the comings and goings of an otherwise absent parent. This anger becomes more understandable when we realize that to a child the presence of an otherwise absent parent always brings forth the specter of anticipated abandonment when the parent leaves. But often as angry as the child is, he or she also needs and wants the comforting presence of both parents. Hence, a child may idealize the absent parent and express his or her anger for the relatively safer and more present parent. The point is that at whatever age loss occurs, there will be specific developmental issues for the child to negotiate.

Idealized Selfobjects

Joanne's self-esteem was tied to her idealized selfobjects. Kohut suggests that children use these selfobjects to enhance their self-esteem. Self-esteem then becomes an organizer of learning, studying, talking, thinking, and self-observing processes. Joanne's selfobject representations of her father were associated with the medical equipment that helped sustain his life. Equipment as a representation of an idealized selfobject had the distinct advantage, in her view, of not feeling. By idealizing that which was nonfeeling, Joanne protected herself from further pain brought about by loss, but it also made her feelings of intimacy anxiety-provoking because she feared the anticipated loss of the loved object.

When Joanne chose a career, she capitalized on her natural talents and skills and became a scientist. Her vocation allowed her to work every day with complex equipment, giving her a sense of purpose and high self-esteem. Part of Joanne's current frustration was that her major source of self-esteem was absent. Joanne quit her job when she first became a mother and, although they are complex, children and husbands are in no way like flasks, petri dishes, or glass tubing. Being a helpmate and mother was interesting but not fulfilling.

Tolerating Intimacy

Throughout the course of caregiving, Joanne found something to bind me as her caregiver to her. This tie proved stronger than any shared religious conviction, although it was not unrelated to her faith. Joanne and I both had undergraduate degrees in science, and we both were parents. Joanne may have come looking for a thin counselor, but she found, in addition, someone who was in her eyes a fellow analytic intellectual who was a parent. The fact that I was no longer interested in pursuing a career in science fueled her wish that maybe she too could find fulfillment outside her chosen field. But more than that, these common ties made her intimate feelings of closeness to me tolerable.

Finding ways to be tolerably close is something that most careseekers do. In that interpersonal intimacy provoked anxiety, Joanne had to find a way to contain the anxiety. Joanne identified with me as an idealized selfobject. In this way she could both enter into a relationship with me and yet still defend against the intolerable anxiety related to her feelings of abandonment. Hence the character of the identification was highly ambivalent. But the fact that I delighted in and enjoyed her telling me about her work-related achievements also enabled her to find the gleam in my eye and use me as a mirroring self-object as well.

Interpersonal closeness with me was also expressed in terms of intellectualization, which was also characteristic of her relationship with her father as a child and the way she sought to be successful in her occupation. Joanne used her intellect as a means to achieve and maintain intimacy. This was one reason

Joanne was having trouble with her children. Not only did their misbehavior make her angry, but they never seemed to have a solid reason for doing "stupid" things. Joanne found reasoning with her children very frustrating.

Intellectualization was also a primary means by which she identified with her father. In Freudian terms, she sublimated her sexual wish for her father and transformed her wish into a desire to have father in an acceptable and non–anxiety-provoking way.

While I am not an ardent believer in penis envy as defined in classical analytic thought, I do subscribe to the notion that children concretize the meaning of maleness and to some degree the meaning of power in their relationship with their father. For Joanne, science was characterized by both maleness and power. Science, as she conceived of it, was a man's domain, and her being a scientist was like being an invader (as opposed to explorer) of foreign territory. In terms of her self-esteem, being close to other scientists, especially male authorities, and being able to "carry off" the invasion increased her self-esteem. It also contributed to her dislike of other women in her field, whom she regarded with suspicion.

Joanne carried with her a vague notion that she did not belong in science. She also felt that if she did her job well enough, she might earn a place for herself. But she exacted such high demands from herself that she could not live up to them. In her efforts to be "perfect," she made errors that she "knew" would disappoint her male boss. With great shame she left her job, not because she had failed, but because she could not live with disappointing her boss, who, Joanne said, bore an uncanny resemblance to her father. Shortly afterward she began a family, but the feelings of shame, frustration, and failure dampened the new joys of being a mother.

In significant ways, Joanne fled her vocation because she felt she did not fit in, but when she left she also left the major source of her self-esteem. Being a scientist was a way to be close to her idealized father-representation, to save him, to keep him to herself. When she left her vocation, she had to grieve for the loss of that closeness as well. All the grief that had never been dealt with, all the sadness and guilt that had been repressed, suddenly began to make their presence known in the form of depression. Living with everyday crises and finding pleasure in her relationships with her spouse and children distracted and protected her from its full expression for a while, but now the last child was leaving her and venturing out, leaving her to grieve over loss again. Hence all the old associated feelings of unresolved grief and loss returned. In classic terms this process can be understood as the return of the repressed.

Joanne joined herself to her scientific occupation as an attempt to derive feelings of power and intimacy just as she had sought her idealized selfobject father. Now, in counseling, she sought to join me for these same things; hence, she tried not to disappoint me by being the "perfect" client.

Split Representations

Joanne's idealized selfobject representations of father were split into a strong, angry, punishing, responsible father and a weak, nonfeeling, impotent, non-responsible father. Joanne's sense of personal strength and stability came primarily from the strong father representation. Because the strong, angry selfobject set limits, it was also used to self-regulate Joanne's feelings generally. Joanne could experience her feelings, but only in a tightly controlled manner and never with full force of expression. Hence her anger was experienced as frustration and her joy as a sort of benign well-wishing. She rationalized this by saying that expressing intense emotion was not a responsible thing to do, and her self-esteem was dependent on her abiding by those strict limitations.

Understanding the dimensions and meaning of the spilt idealized representations took many months of patient listening and paying close attention to the transference. Surmising that her father was an important object from the beginning, I paid close attention to the various ways she described him, especially in relation to herself. While asking myself the question, "How is she experiencing my empathy now?" as she talked, I could remain focused on when she drew closer to me, distanced herself from me, or sought to be over against me. I especially began to see that when Joanne drew closer to me, she did so in an attempt to find strength and stability. During these times she expected me to not only be strong and responsible but be angry and punishing as well. When I did not meet these expectations, she generally evoked a memory of her father who did act in such a way. The process of her experiencing her expectations of herself and me made closeness a thing both to be desired (she wished for it) and dreaded (I did not meet all of her expectations of shoring up her self). Hence she was ambivalent. My job at this point was to raise the ambivalence; that is, to make the unconscious process conscious. In this way we surveyed holy ground together.

Joanne experienced her depression as being like a gnawing hunger. She gradually began to understand that her eating binges were an attempt to satisfy physically a need to break limits that had become inappropriate constraints. But the limitations imposed by her idealized selfobjects also gave her a sense of security, safety, and control. Her fear was that without constraint, she would feel completely out of control and cease to be a self. Being this much out of control evoked an anxiety of annihilation. During these times of intense anxiety, Joanne generally turned to food. In caregiving, she gradually turned toward me.

In this case a behavior, such as eating, was a way to resolve the intrapsychic conflict and shore up her self. Eating was the primary way Joanne used to comfort herself when she felt the gnawing presence of depression. Sadly, her depression was so deep that no amount of food could satisfy her need for comfort. Joanne saw her increasing weight as a testimony of her own inability to properly control her world, that is, herself. She also saw her child's entry into kindergarten as the inevitable prophecy of her own falling apart.

The weak, nonfeeling, impotent, and nonresponsible idealized selfobject also played a part in shoring up her self-esteem. This showed up particularly in her never wanting to be the one who was totally responsible. She wanted to be a leader, but she also wanted not to be the final authority. She was happy to be the assistant but never the boss. She said that she could never be good enough. Never being the boss meant she never had to fail in her responsibilities, and she could maintain the fantasy of her perfection. As far as her religion, she thought of herself as a humble "helpmate" to God and to her husband. The underside of that was that her own sense of perfection meant she could easily find flaws in others. While she tried to exempt God and her husband from her "unfailing" scrutiny, she, of course, could not.

My experience with her was similar to others in this respect: Joanne had a knack of telling me how I ought to approach her in counseling. Maybe I should read this or that book. I needed to be especially sensitive to "people" when they felt a particular way. This whole issue came clearly into focus over her concerns about her steadily increasing weight. Joanne had expected that counseling would raise her self-esteem. Her logic presumed that her having higher self-esteem would stop her overeating and she would lose weight. Somehow telling me about her overeating was supposed to magically reduce her appetite without any exercise or reduction of caloric intake on her part.

I was concerned that one of her major goals for counseling was not being met, but somehow I was also angry about it. For about six sessions, Joanne would begin with how depressed she was because she had gained one or two pounds. Every day she tied her feeling good about herself to what happened when she stood on the scales. If she had gained, she felt depressed; if she had remained the same, she felt frustrated; if she had lost, she felt better. One day, I lost my patience and told her to just put the scales away: Don't look at them if they upset you so much. Of course, she had a score of reasons why she could not. As we returned to this incident many times, I finally came to understand that it was not only that Joanne wanted me to feel as frustrated as she felt, so I could be more empathic, but that she was trying to make me into the weak, impotent, and nonresponsible idealized selfobject so I could support her self-esteem this way too.

The main difference between my response as such a selfobject and the representation of her father was that I got angry, while her father either cut off his feelings completely or exploded. He was either nonfeeling or dangerous. I was neither. Please understand what this meant for Joanne. As mentioned earlier, Joanne split her idealized selfobjects into those who embodied being strong, angry, punishing, and responsible and those who embodied being weak, non-feeling, impotent, and nonresponsible. These selfobjects were based with her childhood experience primarily with her father. Joanne used me as an idealized selfobject, except her experience with me did not conform to her previous experience. When I experienced being weak, impotent, and nonresponsible, I got angry, but I was also able to be angry without punishing her.

Over time, Joanne integrated her experience with me into her memories of her father. Later on in counseling, Joanne remembered a time when she saw tears in her father's eyes. This hitherto forgotten incident was significant, because from it she gleaned that there could be strength in vulnerability and risk taking. She also integrated this insight into her relationship with her children. She came to understand that punishing a child appropriately could be a responsible act but was not necessarily an angry act. She felt freer to risk and trust that her children would still love her if she set limits for them.

Representations of God

As Joanne's idealized representations of her father were split, so too were her representations of God. God was strong, forbidding, punishing, and responsible. Joanne reasoned it out this way: God was the terrible creator. He—and for Joanne God was a "he"—was to be held in awe and treated with utmost respect. As a religious caregiver, she expected me to be familiar with God and language about God. During the course of counseling she talked about her religion to show me how pious she was, thus maintaining her image of herself as a perfect client, but at other times she seemed genuinely puzzled by God.

Richard Bruehl, one of my colleagues and former supervisors, suggested that when careseekers talk about God within the context of the counseling relationship, they are always talking in some way to you, the caregiver. In my experience this is true. Careseekers may also talk to the God of their heritage, but on the holy ground treaded upon in caregiving, you, the caregiver, are God's closest manifestation. You represent God in the here and now. Despite your failings and perhaps even your feelings about the matter, the careseeker puts his or her faith in you. But for healing to be optimal, you the caregiver must have your faith securely rooted. You must have a source of replenishment, a place where your soul is restored. If not, the daily toil of caregiving will drain you dry. It is as though you must know where the living water is in order to keep the holy ground fertile.

While one of Joanne's representations of God was strong, forbidding, punishing, and responsible, another representation of God was weak, nonfeeling (as opposed to inviting), impotent, and nonresponsible. The strong God was named God the Father, and the weak God was his child Jesus.

Joanne found confirmation of her representations of God in her religion. To be in God's will meant to abide by rules that were conceived of as restraints on behavior. "Going to heaven" was a reward for pious living. Joanne's problem was that she could never feel that she was pious enough. She did not read her Bible daily as she thought she should and as her father had done. She struggled daily with the "sin of gluttony," as she called her weight problem, vilifying it. She felt she obviously did not have the "fruits of the Spirit" because she did not have self-control. She labored under the guilt and shame of being unworthy, yet she secretly harbored pride in her humility.

Joanne concluded that if salvation is "once and for all," then she must not even be saved. Yet, being a "good" Christian also carried with it the anxiety of ending up as her father did—dead—or as she herself was, empty and abandoned.

God the Exalted Father

Joanne's representations of God were in large part an exalted father. But "exalted" here means that her God was not just a larger-than-life representation of her father but a prototypic representation of her father. Joanne's God was not just a representation of what her relationship with her father was or what she wished it had been; it was also a model of what ought to be or what should be.

As a selfobject, Joanne's representation of father provided limitations and gave form and meaning to her feelings by controlling them in what was deemed a "responsible" way. As a prototypic selfobject, Joanne's God ordained that these things ought to be. But for Joanne, limitation became bondage and control became stifling. Joanne disavowed the full expression of her feelings and repressed her rage and rebellion, which left her feeling stymied.

At the same time, the idealized selfobject that was characterized as weak, nonfeeling, nonresponsible, and impotent became prototypic of what was a good and acceptable self in God's sight. This was represented by Jesus, who, while not really comforting, was at least not anxiety-provoking.

The idealized selfobject that was characterized as powerful, forbidding, angry, and responsible became prototypic of who God the Father was, but not who Joanne was. These feelings produced anxiety and were disavowed by her. For Joanne, the "real" Joanne could never be powerful, forbidding, angry, or fully responsible, but she never had to because God was.

These idealized selfobjects became manifest in the transference. They were part of her ambivalence toward trusting me enough to feel close to me. As a religious authority I was, in her eyes, powerful, angry, and in some ways responsible for her. When she saw me as a powerful figure it meant that I was capable of healing her. To Joanne, my authority made me responsible in some ways for her. Yet she feared my inevitable anger, so she acted with compliance. At this stage, any interpretation I suggested was met with her gratitude, and she would often begin sessions by saying how much what I had said in the last session had helped her. While I was glad that she seemed to be taking the sessions "home" with her, I also began to notice that the relationship was not proceeding in the direction of greater depth and scope. She said she was being helped, but we were not really dealing with her frustrations.

After this scenario went on for a while, Joanne tried a different tactic. She was so sure that I must be angry with her that she began trying to provoke it. And, of course, she picked a vital and vulnerable spot in me. She became delinquent in paying my fee. I still did not get angry, but I quietly reminded her of our original agreement that missing payment meant that we would have to discontinue our relationship. By this time we had a strong working alliance, so that my restatement of the policy had the desired effects; namely, she paid her bill, and she tried to understand why she suddenly had begun this behavior. The fact, in her eyes, that I could make her "pay up" only made me more powerful.

A tragic element in her representations of God was that there was little room for forgiveness. Joanne carried a lot of shame, but her Jesus lacked compassion, so he was unable to empathize with her sufferings. Jesus could not forgive, because he could not feel her need. God the Father was a punishing parent. God the Father might see her need, but he could only offer mercy, not forgiveness, and being capricious, God might not even offer that. Joanne thought that God knew what was fair and right, although he could not really be counted on to do it. He would know when she did or did not read her Bible or attend church, and while he might know her intentions and motivations, he might or might not choose to punish her or her family. Most likely he would temper her punishment so that she would be able to withstand it.

All these associated thoughts and feelings came to the fore in one of our sessions. One of her acquaintances had a baby that was born dead. Although this woman was not a close friend, Joanne was overwhelmed with grief. The death of this innocent child took Joanne to new depths of depression. While Joanne was in much pain, at least she had moved out of her frustration and denial of her own suffering. Joanne was very angry at God for allowing this to happen. As she focused on her anger, I was able to connect with her. My heart began to pound as I sat with her. She began to recall forgotten memories of her own childhood, particularly in relation to her father's death. She then began to heave long sobs. The sadness felt as though it would overwhelm her. In reaction, she began to close herself and try to shut off the pain. "Do I have to feel this all today?" she asked me. "Do you?" I asked. "I felt you with me," she replied. "Somehow your being there helped me remember." There was a long silence. Then she said, "How innocent I really was. It was not my fault. Those times I wished he would just go away and leave me alone. I never really wanted him to die."

Joanne left that session and later called me to tell me she was all right. For the next several sessions, she explored this incident, which was a turning point in our therapeutic relationship. Primarily she sought to understand how I was able to be with her in her despair. She also struggled to understand how my presence somehow ameliorated her pain. Thus we entered a new phase in our relationship on holy ground.

Further Exploration of Holy Ground

Joanne's representation of her good and acceptable self as nonfeeling was a powerful resistance to change. But in experiencing intimacy with me, she began to feel more. Although she experienced affirmation of her feelings from me, her feelings scared her. Then a complication arose: she learned that I was pregnant. My pregnancy posed a great dilemma for Joanne. She could no longer represent me as not having sufficient power to help her, because, in her eyes, I carried within me an expression of creative, sexual power—a child.

She also experienced me as a powerful, forbidding, punishing, idealized selfobject. While on one hand she wished to be close to me, on the other hand she pushed me away with anger and jealousy. Over time, we came to understand that part of her wished she was that baby inside of me. Her fantasies involved feeling safe, nurtured (fed), and protected. Another part of her, however, felt afraid, rejected, and controlled. Somehow she felt threatened by my pregnancy and replaced by my unborn child.

It took months before Joanne could vocalize her wishes and fears. At first, she just worried about the baby. She seemed overly concerned about whether it would live or die. For several sessions she talked about babies and young children she knew who had died. Joanne became increasingly sad and began reporting symptoms of depression (increased intake of food, sleeplessness, a decreased interest in seeing friends). Given her previous patterns, I suspected that she had redirected feelings of anger and fear toward herself and sealed them over with an emotional layer of guilt.

I encouraged her to explore her feelings. What she termed guilt was really shame. She was both angry and afraid that there was something terribly wrong with her, and she felt largely responsible for being abandoned by her father. She felt like a guilty little girl because she harbored a secret joy that her father did die. Joanne's need to feel safe, nurtured, and protected by him was inevitably frustrated. Instead, she felt afraid, rejected, and controlled. The upshot of her shame was that she was also robbed of joy, of the passion of living. All she really wanted was for someone to find that little girl and help her understand that she did not kill her father, and that wishing never makes it so.

As we got closer to that little girl, Joanne's ambivalence toward me intensified. Her needs to feel accepted and affirmed sparked fantasies of being inside me as my unborn child, and indeed, I had maternal feelings toward her. There were times that her feelings toward me were so intense she feared she might be gay. During these times we talked and processed her sexual feelings. While she sought assurances from me, I pointed out to her that her depression was lifting. The more she found nurturing from me, the less she binged. This was all true, she said, but still it was scary.

Empathic Failure

My pregnancy meant that I would have to leave Joanne. I discussed with her my decision that after the birth I was going to quit working for a while and refer any remaining clients. This forced Joanne to deal with the reality of impending loss. Her response was to deny the significance of our therapeutic relationship, claiming that it had always been "just temporary," meaning lacking substance.

Joanne understood my pregnancy as a traumatic empathic failure. In order to deal with her feelings of abandonment, she denied that therapy was helping her. After all, her weight had steadily increased throughout therapy. She also intellectualized our relationship by saying that, given the nature of therapy, "of course" it must end. But through experiencing expected loss of me as an idealized selfobject, she repeated what she did when she lost her father; she redirected her attention from her feelings to the apparatus. This meant she became inordinately interested in the mechanics and techniques of counseling. This shift took the form of her reading "self-help" books and asking me questions about the techniques I used. This was a resistance to further intimacy, because it focused her away from her further self-revelation.

Reading self-help books and asking questions may not necessarily be resistances, but in this case they were. Joanne used them as barriers between us, rather than gateways toward a therapeutic relationship of greater depth and scope. Reading and asking questions could also be understood as an attempt to be more like me. There may have been some shifting of the transference toward twinship dynamics. Yet her attempts at identification were defensive, because they led her away from increased self-understanding.

Joanne's Mother

Finally, Joanne began to believe that her frustration, as she called it, was an expression of hostility and anger. While she denied any anger toward me, she did realize that there were characteristics of her father that angered her. As she increasingly touched upon feelings of abandonment, she began to say that she hated that part of herself that was angry with her father. Invariably, when Joanne would be just about ready to look at this hated part of herself, she would feel anxious and then shut off her feelings. Then she would also say that she was fortunate to have such an understanding mother. Recalling memories of an understanding mother was not only an attempt to soothe her anxiety and shut off her feelings (repression), but a turning away from me as well.

At first I simply pointed out the pattern of her responses. Later, I called to her attention that she had shut off her feelings. The more I asked her to focus, the more she fled to soothing representations of mother—until one holiday when her mother came to visit, and Joanne confronted the reality of her mother. During the next session, Joanne expressed much disappointment concerning her mother. Her mother had such high expectations of who Joanne should be. Joanne felt the force of her mother's rejection and non-acceptance.

Joanne then gave a more balanced picture of her mother. No doubt her mother had been soothing to some degree, but Joanne perceived other, seemingly more pertinent, features of her character. Joanne described her mother as an appendage of her father. Sure she had strengths or she would not have able to raise her children as well as she did, but while father was alive, mother was just another child in the family.

Joanne struggled with her ambivalence toward her mother. On one hand, her mother held the family together, but on the other, she never had enough time for any one child. As Joanne was trying to understand her mixed feelings toward her mother, I asked her how she brought those feelings into our relationship. Joanne had been aware that she looked to me as a "stand in" for her mother from time to time, but my question seemed to surprise her. At first she said it seemed to be a confusing question, but she quickly proceeded to answer. She experienced a great swell of feeling and began to cry. She then confessed how jealous she was of my baby. Her fantasy was that being in therapy was like being inside a womb where not only was she safe but she did not have to compete for my attention. She said she felt appreciated and understood here and she wondered where she would go to feel that way once we terminated. Somehow being with me held her together. The thought of being without me caused her great anxiety.

As Joanne spoke, she struggled to hold her representations of me together. While I was "bad" for abandoning her, I was "good" for wanting to be a responsible parent and devote myself totally (from Joanne's point of view) to my unborn child. While I could have asked her who abandoned her, I chose to ask who was she abandoning. Ever since the beginning of therapy, Joanne had spoken of herself as the one left, by her father, her mother, and even her own children. In my experience a person who fears and expects abandonment often abandons others first in order to protect themselves from what they perceive as inevitable pain. Joanne had never thought of this. In one sense I was asking her to identify with me in a new way. In another sense I was curious about her current relationships, particularly her marriage.

Many persons marry partners in order to fill their own childhood needs that were unmet by parents. I was also aware of the sequence of Joanne's relationships: first, idealized father; second, idealized male teachers; third, idealized male boss; and then marriage. I wondered how Joanne idealized her husband and what had happened in that relationship. I wondered whether her husband had abandoned her in some way, too, and if not, whether she had abandoned him.

Praying for the Caregiver

My question of who she was abandoning made her bolt. She changed the subject completely and never acknowledged my asking it. At the beginning of the next session (which was about six months into therapy), Joanne said that she was praying for me. While clients sometimes say this to me and while I appreciate prayers, the timing of Joanne's praying made me a little suspicious. Why me, now? What did this say about her experience of my empathy?

While she did not share with me the content of her prayers, I believe it was a way Joanne was reaching for God's help. My fantasy was that if she perceived that I had failed her or abandoned her, she was sending in God as the "heavy hitter." But this also puzzled me. Why would she reach to God? Her God seemingly only brought her pain, unless God also brought her closer to some idealized selfobject, perhaps her religious father. And of course, I was a religious professional.

Joanne regarded prayer as a dangerous activity. She believed that once a person "turned things over to the Lord," one could never quite be sure what God would do. Yet prayer was a way of raising her self-esteem, because a constant prayer life was one of the things she admired about her father and a behavior she attributed to me. He had prayed every day without fail. While she sought to identify with her father by sharing with him the conviction that prayer was essential to living, she encountered another problem. She did not pray daily. In her mind she did not pray well enough, often enough, or unselfishly enough. In short, she did not do it perfectly.

As we sought to understand her ambivalence toward God and talking with God in prayer, Joanne discovered that she not only respected God, as opposed to loving God, but she dreaded God. God could see things about her she could not. Working on the assumption that when the careseeker talks about God in the session, he or she is also talking to the caregiver, I wondered if she was saying something to me, particularly in regard to my question during the last session.

As she talked about God, Joanne expressed both fear and pain. She longed to be closer to God, but somehow it was painful too. Joanne wondered if the pain was worth being related to God. I used this remark to bring her back into the room with me. "You seem to be feeling some fear and pain in regard to this." "Yes," she said, and she heaved a long sigh. "It is just hard to be seen when I don't always know what I am showing . . . you." "Are we talking about the last session?" I asked. "It is frustrating. No, it frightens me to see that I abandon people too," she said.

From here she went on to talk of how she both wanted to be like her father and feared being like him. She saw some of her fears realized with her children—that is, her unyielding attempts to reason with and discipline her children. But she also saw it in relation to her husband. He was the one she abandoned out of fear, but also anger. She then launched into a lengthy discussion of her sexual history with her husband.

As Joanne's God represented her wish to be with and like her father, God also represented her fears of being with and like him. God brought her closer to her father, but at the same time kept her safely away from him. Perhaps Joanne feared what it might mean to be with or to have her father. In any case, she used God as a barrier, a defense against the anxiety of having sexual feelings. This became more clear as we progressed.

Praying for me at that particular stage of her care could have meant many things, and it did. It meant associating me more closely with her father and hence herself, and it also meant protecting herself from me as well. It meant she cared for me, but that she must not care too much nor risk losing me. Just what part the sexual feelings played, we never fully understood. Perhaps she had sexual feelings toward me in some fashion. Perhaps she used her religiosity to suppress her sexual feelings. Perhaps feelings of anger and fear were associated with her sexual relationships. Perhaps she was replaying the Oedipal drama. In any case, praying for me meant putting our relationship in some relation to God.

As we struggled to focus on her feelings, Joanne gradually realized that she did not have to be perfect. While she experienced this insight as a relief and as a lifted burden, she immediately became anxious, because she did not have an alternate way of being. As Joanne explored her experiences of making and abiding by her own rules, she gradually realized that being flexible and tolerating, for example, the interruptions of her children, might not mean she was an utter failure as a Christian or parent.

The issue of failing was especially keen when it came to her weight. Every morning she stepped on the scales. Obviously, she did not follow my suggestion to put the scales away. If she had not gained a pound, she felt great. If she had gained, she felt frustrated all day, because she had failed. She tried to follow diets, which to her were rules laid down by thin people, but she could not "stick" to them. She finally realized that she had tied her entire self-concept and self-esteem to the bathroom scales. Not surprisingly, this made her very angry. But her anger, while associated with her attitude toward the scales, was more directly related to having to look at herself as she was. Confronting the "ugly" parts of herself was difficult and also made her angry with me. After all, I enabled, precipitated, and in her eyes, compelled her to look at herself.

Mirroring Selfobject

Under Joanne's anger was fear—fear of seeing flaws in herself and, parenthetically, me. During this phase of our relationship, she had much trouble looking me in the eye. When I drew this to her attention, she began to recall memories of her mother.

Joanne began to use me more consistently as a mirroring selfobject; that is, she began to search for the gleam in my eye. Further, her fear raised so much anxiety that she used me to perceive that she was fearful, and to find what it meant. This is what I mean: as Joanne spoke of the "ugly" parts of herself, she would begin to feel anxious. This anxiety would invariably cut off her foresight and block her from feeling further. As I resonated with her as she spoke, I noticed that my heart would begin to beat faster. From sitting with her for many sessions, I knew that my quickened heart rate probably was an empathic response to her feelings of fear. I would then mirror my response by saying something like, "You seem to be fearful." She would usually heave a long sigh and become aware of that feeling. Memories would then surface.

The memories that generally surfaced had to do with herself as a little girl who felt very angry, weak, and out of control. She felt punished by what God had "dealt" her, and she felt guilt over her "irresponsible" expressions of hostility. Believing that she was also talking to me, I asked her how she brought these feelings of being punished into the counseling room with her. At this point she began to cry and lament that my pregnancy meant that I would leave her. To Joanne, my carrying a new life in my womb somehow meant that I was replacing her, that is, killing her chances at getting "better."

When my empathy proved not quite "good enough," Joanne would usually turn to memories of her mother as an attempt to bring forth a soothing, mirroring selfobject. But she was angry with her mother as well. Because her father died, the mother and children were put in dire financial straits. Joanne had to wear hand-me-downs and accept charity from people she did not like. This made her lose face with her peers. Her self-esteem was very low, in part, because she felt cheated of her "rightful" place with her peers. Not only that, but her father's death meant that she had to change schools and lose her friends. Somehow she was also angry at her mother for not providing her with another father.

When she actually did seek solace from her mother, mother became un-available, because she had to go to her job. To Joanne, mother had no time for her and appeared unsympathetic. Joanne felt abandoned again. Not having a sufficient amount of mothering and having lost significant peer relationships meant that she clung even tighter to her idealized representations of her father as strong and responsible. She would become strong and responsible. Hand-me-downs were awful, but at least they were new to her. She could sympathize with people who felt cheated and disliked, because she experienced those things too. And she made several promises to herself, one being that she would never desert her children by having a job outside the home.

To Joanne's credit, she tried to turn her tragedies into something better, but this meant that she felt any perceived tragedy, including those of others, as a narcissistic injury. In a sense, she was always looking for tragedies so as to avoid them, but, of course, this meant that she always found them.

To be responsible and thus identify with her idealized image of father meant that she listened to other people's problems and took them on herself inappropriately. Thus, Joanne experienced grief and heartache for others but not for herself. That is, by focusing on other people's hurts, she avoided her own hurt rather than use them to better understand her own. This puzzled both Joanne and me for a long time. On one hand, she was a deeply compas-sionate person, but on the other, she could not display compassion toward herself.

Being Nourished on Holy Ground

Finally, Joanne gave up. She decided that others would just have to be respon-sible for themselves. This was reflected in her attitude toward her child in kin-dergarten. He would just have to get along without her. The fact that he seemed to being doing so well without her was bittersweet. Joanne said she was just tired of trying to "be all things to all people." This terminology was significant, because this was how she (and how the apostle Paul) described the church.

Joanne even felt responsible for God. Not directly, because God was still very distant and threatening, but through serving in God's house, the church, Joanne could take care of the "small" things so God would not have to be bothered with them. This scenario was how Joanne's mother had cared for the father. Being a "helpmate" meant doing things so that the father, and by ex-tension, God, would not have to. But an unintended consequence was that Joanne made her relationship with her husband part of the pattern. And just as Joanne's father and God were distant and threatening, so her representations of her husband had become increasingly integrated into that prototypic idealized selfobject. This means that the distance she had experienced from her father, the distance she experienced from God, the fears of intimacy which made them threatening, and the energy she invested in keeping them at a "safe" distance became part of her relationship with her husband.

A result of counseling was that the constant focus on herself made Joanne very tired, and eventually she felt she had no alternative but to try something new. Typically, she began to search for an intellectual solution. The solution she settled on was an interesting compromise between focusing on the mechanics (so she could do it right) and avoiding feelings of failure and anger. Joanne decided she could live a more satisfying life if she could conceive of her life as "practice."

Practicing also became a dominant metaphor for therapy. It was a compromise between having to be perfect and expecting to fail. It was also an interesting integration of both her and my religious orientations. According to Joanne's faith, one is "saved once and for all." To Joanne this meant one had better do it right the first time or risk living in the "outer darkness," that is, hell. In my religious tradition we have a notion of "going on to perfection." I am not going to discuss the theological merits or implications of either tradition. All I want to underscore is that of all the things Joanne could have picked out of either tradition, these were the ones she picked, and that she used them to her psychological advantage. By "practicing" she could both be on her way toward doing it right, yet not be expected to accomplish it, and still be a faithful Christian.

The metaphor of "practicing" enabled Joanne to find a new approach. By holding her fears of failure and demands for perfection at bay, it freed her to succeed. Practicing meant that she could try something new without expecting to do it perfectly. It meant that she did not have to feel totally responsible, because she had not yet "arrived." It meant that she could "experiment" with her feelings, and thus she did not have to be so afraid of what might happen if she expressed her feelings. This metaphor tied in nicely with her scientific background and thus preserved a tie to her idealized selfobjects, yet it also tied her to me as a practicing professional. Joanne's association of practicing being on a diet meant that she did not have to fail, and her self-imposed eating limitations did not feel so much like punishment.

Joanne's association of practicing to God was also interesting. As a practicing Christian, she did not have to fear God's anger and consequent punishment for her own expressions of anger and irresponsibility. Moving toward perfection meant going in God's direction and that was all God expected.

Joanne began to understand that for her practicing did not mean that she was irresponsible or that she denied her responsibility. It did mean, however, that she was not alone in her responsibility or anything else. When Joanne reached this insight something happened. She remembered that once her father had told her he loved her. Tears welled up in her eyes as she spoke of how lonely she felt and how much she missed her father. Joanne showed me the depth of her grief. I cried too and felt both sorrow for her loss and loneliness, yet I also knew that this could be a new beginning for Joanne. She had removed a major obstacle to being intimate with others. Now, perhaps, she could receive in a relationship as well as give.

I was not sure, at the time, what Joanne would make of my tears. She simply said that my tears made hers easier to bear. In this instance she not only used me to mirror her feelings, but as an idealized selfobject as well, a source of comfort with which she could momentarily merge. In so doing she felt my concern for her and she did not feel alone.

Shortly thereafter, Joanne began to talk more about God. God was still a problem for Joanne, now, more than ever, because God could be different too. She had spent most of her life doing her religious duties in order to avoid God. Now what if she did not have to? This concern made Joanne very confused. Did it mean that possibly she needed to change more than she had realized?

Sharing the Fruit

If one conceives of caregiving as a process with a beginning, middle, and end, then Joanne's had a very long end. She spent several months trying to say good-bye. This is not to say that she spent those months trying to simply leave me, but that it took her that amount of time to decide what she was going to do with what she had gained. For Joanne it was important for her to decide on a "next step" before she left.

She still expressed disappointment in me for not solving her weight problem, but she let me know that I was still a "good" counselor. In some ways, I was sorry too. I wished that enhanced self-esteem could have motivated her to lose weight, but I also thought that if she really wanted to lose weight she was going to have to do more than come and talk about it with me. I was an appropriate companion for part of Joanne's journey toward wholeness, but not for this part. In my opinion she needed the support of a group. I told her so.

Joanne did not like my comment at all! She thought I was trying to terminate our relationship so I could go ahead and have my baby. While her logic was less than convincing, I nevertheless pressed for her to join a support group for her weight. This brought forth all her fears of being a peer, or in technical terms, having twinship relationships.

I tried to assure her that I had her best interest at heart. She knew this and said so, but her anger toward me finally became focused enough for us to deal with. How could I ever empathize with her when I was thin? Of course I was not thin, because all pregnant women, myself included, gain weight. How could I be strong and available to her when I was subject to all the mood swings and morning sickness of a pregnant woman? I wondered a little about this, too, and in our talking about it, we drew closer. Increasingly, Joanne recalled her own pregnancies and began to look to me as a twin. As she did so, she both dissipated her need to rebel against me and deny her need for a support group and at the same time prepare herself to join one.

Eventually Joanne began to recognize that I was portraying reality to her. I bore her no ill will. I was not punishing her by leaving her or suggesting she leave me before she was ready. Support groups could work to help her with her weight, if that was truly her goal. While she began, perhaps, to hurt me by denying me the pleasure of helping her further and thus hurting my professional pride, she slowly found that leaving would not be easy. She invested a lot in our relationship, and she found that she still needed me; further, she found she wanted to need me.

Counseling was a safe place where she both gave and received. She gave by investing her time, money, and intimate aspects of herself. But she also found solace, comfort, and a sense of peace by being with me. In these ways she received. The task was for her to find ways she could receive from others—in short, replace me.

Finally, Joanne came to counseling and announced that this was the last session. There was finality in her voice. She said that she cared enough about me to let me go. Parenthetically, she also said that she had added up how much counseling had cost her. She had spent enough. Actually, she said she had spent more than she had anticipated. Still what she had gained, she said, was worth it. (Perhaps she was referring to her weight gain as well.) She felt more comfortable disciplining her children. She was at peace with her youngest not needing her so much, although, she added, she would always "be there" for her children (probably whether they wanted it or not). She found herself able to share new aspects of herself with those closest to her. She said even her husband noticed that the edge to her voice was gone and that she seemed different somehow. I could not help feeling that she was also saying good-bye to her father in some way. She said "of course," because she forgave him for abandoning her. As for me, this good-bye was not final, because our relationship was a part of her. She felt she could call me if she needed to. She asked me if I was sad to see her go. I said yes, but that I understood. She then presented me with a lovely gift for the baby. I was deeply touched and let her go.

There were no tears or lamentations, only a silent understanding between us that she received my blessing in her leave-taking. She had enough for now and it was good enough. There would always be new problems and issues to think about and sort through, but she now carried with her the assurance that she did not have to be alone. The fruit she garnered was a greater capacity for kindness, patience, and goodness toward both self and others, and a greater capacity to share herself intimately.

Conclusions

Through caregiving, Joanne increased her capacity to empathize and sustain relationships of greater depth and scope. But caregiving never ends neatly. There is always more that can be done, more insights to offer, more meaning to create and share. There is also a limit to what most people can stand. Most people can stand a relationship of only so much depth and scope. While it helps for caregivers to have a great capacity for intimacy with careseekers, caregivers must also be able to discern not only their own limitations but also those of their clients.

Most people can stand on holy ground only for so long. Being in communion with what ultimately matters is both an awe-inspiring and dreadful experience. We religious professionals tend to act as though inspiration is all there is. We tend to overlook the dreadful and painful consequences. While no mortal can look into the face of God, we mortals also have problems looking into the self for fear of our own narcissistic injury. If, however, we endure and peek flirtatiously, quite often we find not just injury but pardon, not just despair but hope, not just anxiety but empathy.

I want to suggest that what we find while on holy ground is of little value unless it is shared with others. In this way, our own treading on holy ground comes to fruition.

~ 5 ~

Epilogue

STANDING, SURVEYING, AND being nourished on holy ground and sharing its fruit are ways of understanding the depth and scope of intimacy caregivers and careseekers experience. It also gives direction and focus to the caregiver's elegant tool of understanding and interpretation, empathy.

In the first chapter we saw that the caregiver enters into the inner world of the careseeker through empathy. The caregiver journeys with the careseeker toward holy ground in an attempt to find what is most common to us all, our humanity, with our frailties, limitations, and sufferings, to be sure, but also with our human capacity for acceptance and affirmation. Standing on holy ground means acknowledging our search for the profound companionship of the Divine Other. This acknowledgment, however, also entails the companionship of empathic human others as well.

In the second chapter we saw that surveying holy ground can be a profound experience for both caregiver and careseeker. Surveying entails the quest for lost wholeness and the inevitable disappointment that complete wholeness is only a fantasy. Yet the possibility for greater wholeness lures one to take steps of faith. As one's interpersonal relationships proceed in the direction of greater depth and scope, one many find further conflict, yet one can be transformed through greater insight and have a clearer grasp of what kinds of companionship one wants, what counts as love and care to the self, what soothes, and what provokes anxiety.

In the third chapter we saw how a careseeker can be nourished on holy ground specifically by the experience of the evoked companion par excellence. While the evoked companion is a product of human development, it is also central to the self's sense of its own well-being. The individual's God, which may or may not resemble the God of a faith community, nevertheless embodies the ultimate worth and value of self and others. Hence if someone experiences his or her God as problematic, there can be profound reverberations in the self's interpersonal relations, including the self's own attempts to soothe itself. This is not to say, however, that God is only an evoked companion, but to say that we understand a person's God through the lens of that person's developmental history and expectations of the future.

The hope in counseling is that being nourished on holy ground by the caregiver's empathy will help the careseeker's relationships to undergo transformation. If so, his or her relationship with God will undergo transformation as well. I do not mean to imply, however, that one's relationship with God will ever come to be conflict-free. There are always elements of inspiration, awe, and dread in relating to God, but finding acceptance makes judgment, even God's, tolerable.

In the fourth chapter we went with Joanne and her caregiver as Joanne stood on, surveyed, and was nourished by holy ground. But caregiving involves not only traveling to holy ground but departing with the fruit of the journey; that is, an increased capacity to be empathic with self and others in the direction of greater depth and scope.

One might ask: Why leave the holy ground if it is such a wonderful place? Does leaving mean one cannot return? Holy ground, as I understand it, is not like the biblical Garden of Eden, that is, that once one partakes of the knowledge of good and evil, one's reentry is forever barred. It is rather that there is a limit to what most people can stand. People, as tragic as it may be, can stand relationships of only so much depth and scope, even, or perhaps especially, with God. People can experience holy ground only for so long.

Why is it that mortals cannot look into the face of God? While there may be a multitude of reasons, one reason is what we fear seeing. We fear our own narcissistic injury. We fear being shattered, torn apart, wounded to the quick; we fear self-annihilation. Whether that fear is justified is another question. Let me just say that in most pictures of the crucifixion I have seen, Christ's eyes are downcast. Perhaps even in God's most self-imposed vulnerability (Christ on the cross) we still cannot face looking into the eyes of God. We fear seeing the gleam in God's eye for what it will reveal about us.

But while there is anxiety, there is also a yearning to commune with God. Many careseekers, while they may be unable to commune much with anyone or experience great ambivalence at the thought, still yearn to be a part of God. In caregiving, the caregiver's hope is that they will find us, the caregivers, as a gateway or path toward a deeper and more variegated relationship with God.

The Question of God

How can God be real to a person when God cannot be seen, touched, or heard like real people? This book has explored this question primarily with a psychological focus. The three major sources of ideas presented in this book—Rizzuto, Kohut, and Stern—stand firmly on psychological ground. Rizzuto's theory points to the fact that individuals' God-representations have pre-Oedipal origins. I used Kohut's concept of selfobject as a lens through which to view his self psychology. I used Stern's ideas to refine Kohut's core concept of selfobject and to examine some developmental aspects of empathy in order to come to a clearer notion of how God might be understood as a substitute selfobject. Using these sources, I suggest that God may be psychologically understood as an evoked companion par excellence. But this analysis raises further questions and has some further implications both psychological and theological that I would like to foreground.

Reconstruction or Cure?

Is it curative or only reconstructive for a person to experience God as an evoked companion par excellence? This question is important to those of us with a more psychological "bent." Thus I will now address this question more technically than in the previous chapters.

Reconstruction is the dynamic-genetic formulation of the individual's reactions. I understand reconstruction as does Kohut, namely, a first step toward cure. It is only a first step, but it is a necessary step. Reconstructions not only enrich the individual's empathy toward the self, but they strengthen the trust in the reality and reliability of the bond with the caregiver. Reconstructions demonstrate the therapist's understanding of the client. Experiences with the evoked companion par excellence can offer careseekers a feeling of empathic understanding that they might not have otherwise.

Such experiences give a person new insight. The hallmarks of an insight may include a burst of creative energy, a sense that "things click" or have fallen "into place." While insight includes understanding, it also includes "working through"; that is, integration into one's daily living, presumably leading to relationships of greater depth and scope.

Cure means new psychological structure. In self psychology this means new and more appropriate selfobjects replace archaic selfobjects. The essence of cure is the person's newly acquired ability to identify and seek appropriate selfobjects (mirroring, idealized, and twinship) as they present themselves in realistic surroundings, and be sustained by them.

Can an experience with one's God lead to cure? If someone's experience with his or her God as an evoked companion par excellence enables real relationships or greater depth and scope, or if the experiences of his or her God

lead to identifying and seeking appropriate selfobjects as they present themselves in everyday surroundings, then, yes, such experiences are curative. They
lead the person toward greater healing and wholeness. If, however, experience
with one's God thwarts or prevents real relationships of greater depth and
scope, such experiences are not curative.

Using this criterion for cure, I suggest that Joanne's experiences were curative, not in any final or ultimate way, but in that she gleaned from her therapy
the assurance that she did not have to be alone. She had more empathy for her
children when they disobeyed and more empathy for herself when she disciplined them. She found herself able to share new aspects of herself with those
closest to her, even her husband.

In theological terms, she found some inner peace and was finally able to
forgive her father for abandoning her. This forgiveness then enabled her to
feel secure enough to be vulnerable with those around her. Hence she was able
to give herself in a deeper and richer way to others and, in turn, receive back
from them. True, her God was both an invitation to further intimacy and a
resistance to it, but through caregiving God became for her a more empathic
selfobject.

But there is also John, whom we met in the first chapter. God appeared to
John while he was undergoing drug withdrawal after a long series of traumatic
incidents. God forgave John's guilt and took the pain away. John made the
association between his physical pain and his own guilt. For him, the removal
of pain meant the absence of guilt, as well as the converse: the subsequent
return of pain meant the presence of guilt. Did John leave the hospital to
avoid further insight and interpersonal intimacy with, for example, his successful wife? Since John's recovery was temporary, was John's experience curative or reconstructive? Or is cure ever anything more than limited and
temporary? Was John's disappointment and bitterness toward God a way of
denying John's own responsibility and disappointment concerning his inability, and perhaps unwillingness, to father children? Or did John believe that not
even God could save him? How are we as caregivers to understand John's continued faith in a God who, in John's eyes, failed him?

John's experience with his evoked companion par excellence was reconstructive but not curative. John felt a temporary relief from pain, but then
used his renewed strength to flee further interpersonal intimacy. One can say
that by fleeing from interpersonal intimacy, John in effect cut himself off from
further healing.

God as Prototypic Empathic Failure

Joanne used her God in order to avoid the anxiety of interpersonal intimacy with her caregiver. While Joanne was a monotheist, she had many representations of God. For example God the Parent was represented one way and God the Child another. When avoiding intimacy she especially used the representation of God the Parent, specifically God the Father. God the Father was punishing, dangerous, and anxiety *provoking*. This raises some interesting questions. If God the Parent represented a "disregulation" of the self, to use Stern's term—that is, if it was anxiety provoking rather than soothing or more anxiety provoking than soothing—could such a representation properly be called a selfobject?

Selfobjects are representations of persons who offer the self developmentally appropriate empathic self-regulation. But even though some persons offer the self very poor empathic response, because these same persons do occasionally give *some* empathy, empathic response does become part of the patterning of representation. However, empathy is then minimal and does not regulate the self when the self is faced with anything other than very minimal anxiety. The empathy offered by such a selfobject simply is not good enough.

But could a selfobject be pathogenic? That is, could a selfobject provoke disintegration anxiety rather than ward it off? Kohut does seem to suggest that some archaic selfobjects may be pathogenic. How can this be? Kohut is not clear on this point. I suggest that if one looks at a person's evoked companions par excellence, one may find a clue. These may be understood as prototypic representations: that is, they are models of models. If *not*-good-enough empathic response becomes a dominant part of prototypic representation, the selfobject may become pathogenic. This means that when faced with anxiety that threatens the self, the self experiences it as a threat to the the selfobject as well—that is, fragmentation of the selfobject. Because the self "knows" fragmentation or selfobject failure "ought" to occur, the self responds defensively to (1) ward off selfobject failure and its consequent anxiety, and (2) protect the selfobject from fragmentation so that it can continue to bind up narcissistic wounds. The empathy offered by the selfobject, poor as it might be, is far better than self-fragmentation.

An analogy: If I have a bottle of medicine that counteracts my rare and fatal disease, I will take very good care of it. Even if my medicine has intolerable side effects, I might prefer the pain brought about by my medicine than dying from not taking it. This medicine is rare and costly, and I protect it and guard its whereabouts. Perhaps I even enshrine it in its own special place. Fearing for my own life is bad enough, but now I also fear losing my bottle of medicine. The point is that I will die without the medicine, so I have to take good care of it, even if it means doing bizarre things like building a wall around my house or never leaving the house for fear of thieves. You see, my medicine is my last line of defense against certain death. In some respects my life is in that bottle.

Something similar may occur with a person and his or her pathogenic self-objects. The person may be so afraid of losing self-cohesion that he or she goes to great lengths to protect and defend the selfobjects that are perceived as life-saving. This would be especially true of selfobjects of evoked companions par excellence (such as God) because the self does not have sufficient real relationships available. Hence there is very strong resistance to change.

The self may prefer the anxiety of its own possible fragmentation to the certain fragmentation of its selfobject. Anxiety concerning the self's fragmentation is painful, but anxiety of selfobject fragmentation seems deadly. The presence of a pathogenic selfobject may disregulate the self, but the person feels that fragmentation of the selfobject, albeit pathogenic, may destroy the self. This may provide a clue as to why John could not ask the question that most troubled him. His question was, Did God fail me? John may have preferred carrying inordinate guilt to scrutinizing his God. His God as an evoked companion par excellence may have been his last line of defense against self-disintegration.

Logical Relations between Selfobjects

Can caregivers understand representations of selfobjects, including of God, using logic? It is beyond the scope of this book to debate the structural aspects of representations, although I believe they are structural in some sense. I do want to suggest, however, that representations can be understood as ordered in a logical way. For example, Joanne's representation of God as God the Parent and God the Child (Jesus) can be understood using logical contraries. For Joanne, God the Parent was strong, punishing, antifeeling; God the Child was weak, sacrificing, and nonfeeling. This is to say that for Joanne strong was a logical contrary to weak, punishing was a logical contrary to sacrificing, and antifeeling was a logical contrary to nonfeeling. Not only that, but one part of the pair of contraries cannot be fully understood without the other.

One could also understand Joanne's self-representations using logical contraries as well. To use Sullivan's concepts of the good me, bad me, and not me,

Joanne's representation of her good me was nonfeeling, not responsible, and dependent. Her bad me was depressed or empty, irresponsible, and weak or guilty. Again, nonfeeling is the contrary of feeling depressed or empty, not responsible is the contrary of irresponsible, and dependent is contrary to weak or guilty.

Joanne also disavowed particular representations of herself. These can be understood in a contrary relation to the bad me. Julie disavowed representations of herself as antifeeling, responsible, and strong or not guilty.

What she repressed can be understood as contrary to the good me. This is Sullivan's not me. Joanne repressed feelings of rage, antiresponsibility or rebellion, and independence, which she understood as abandonment.

I suggest that viewing a careseeker's representations using logical relations may aid in entering another's inner construction of meaning. There are at least two ways a caregiver can ascertain these contraries: (1) by patient, empathic listening to the descriptions of the careseeker's selfobjects, and (2) observing the behavior of the careseeker. Psychologist George Kelley's concept of shuttling is helpful to unpack this second point. According to Kelley, when a careseeker changes his or her behavior, the new behavior will often be the opposite of the old behavior. In couple's therapy, we often see the partner who was once the pursuer become the distancer, while the partner who was once the distancer becomes the pursuer. A person may go from keeping secrets, for example, to telling all private information, that is, having no secrets. This flipflop of behavior is shuttling. By observing from what to what, or to whom, the careseeker shuttles, including the associated feelings and memories, the caregiver may ascertain how the careseeker has constructed contraries in his or her inner world.

Gender Representation of God

Is gender designation of God important to a dynamic understanding of personality? Rizzuto points out, as do many other current theorists, that maternal as well as paternal characteristics may go into the God representation "mix." And I assert that people have a narcissistic investment in representing their God with a particular gender. Joanne's God was almost exclusively paternal, almost exclusively an image of Freud's "exalted father." One reason Joanne's representations of God had such a great narcissistic investment was Joanne's lack of benign paternal experience.

One might say that a reason God is represented as predominantly male in this culture is that each person needs a kind, present, and loving father. If a person has an absent father or one who is primarily experienced as punishing and authoritarian, like Joanne's, then that person might represent God as embodying those qualities of a wished-for father.

Following this line of reasoning, one might conjecture one reason there is currently an emphasis on maternal characteristics of God in certain intellectual communities is that those persons are experiencing growing empathic failure from maternal selfobjects. In other words, people may represent God with qualities of a wished-for mother.

Given this argument, one would also have to ask, what if neither parent offered good-enough empathy? What if someone has to embody the qualities of both a wished-for mother and father? These questions are important and need careful study.

As a pastoral counselor, I realize people project many kinds of needs and wishes onto God. A person's God may embody all kinds of relationships and values, which may or may not be congruent with a particular faith community. One then has to ask: What criteria does a careseeker use to evaluate the health, for lack of a better term, of a careseeker's God? In my United Methodist tradition, we use the Wesleyan Quadrilateral: Scripture, tradition, reason, and experience (with an emphasis on Scripture). I want to further suggest that a careseeker's representation of God is "going on toward perfection," to use another Wesleyan phrase, if it facilitates dynamic interpersonal relationships of increasing depth and scope.

One final word on God's gender. Since gender and sexuality are basic parts of who people are and perceive themselves to be, it does not seem surprising that people would need to represent their God as having a particular sexual identity or orientation and that they have deep narcissistic investment in their representations personally, communally, and culturally.

The Importance of the Church

If curative experiences with one's God involve seeking appropriate selfobjects as they present themselves in realistic surroundings and receiving sustenance from them, then it seems obvious to me that one cannot overstate the value of the community of believers, the church.

It also seems that the church would carry some unique responsibilities, one being the recognition that individuals can have very different images of God and that there are a whole host of reasons for these differences, some of which are developmental. Another responsibility or obligation would be to educate people, not so as to eliminate differences, but to bring people into a deeper and richer relationship with their God and, concurrently, with one another. A third responsibility would be to stress the importance of real relationships in communities, and that salvation, if it is to mean anything at all in one's daily living, involves shouldering one another's burdens, not out of guilt, but out of valuing others' self-worth.

Pastoral Caregiving

God as an evoked companion par excellence gives caregivers another way to understand careseekers' language about God. But pastoral caregivers are in a unique position to study the personal meaning that an individual's God has, because expectations and assumptions about God are part and parcel of what it means to be pastoral. As an evoked companion par excellence, a representation of God emerges as a central dynamic in each person's sense of self.

Conceptualizing individuals' God in this way also gives pastoral caregivers a tool that can be used in an interdisciplinary context. For example, in my experience as a pastoral counselor, I have noticed that many people have vivid experiences with God while hospitalized or while a loved one is hospitalized. The stressful nature of hospitalization often means that a person feels totally alone and abandoned. This is just the kind of situation where one would expect to see the appearance of God as an evoked companion par excellence. This understanding can give religious professionals another way to communicate with hospital personnel the psychological needs of the patient.

If people understand God as their "last line of defense," then pastoral caregivers must take language about God very seriously. Empathic listening then becomes the primary mode of operation with careseekers rather than preaching at or lecturing to.

Pastoral Theology

Pastoral theology arises out of intense human need for an interpersonal relationship with God. Given the context of crisis that accompanies careseekers as they present themselves to caregivers for care, the theology that emerges out of such encounters is messy and occasional. Quite often a careseeker's relationship with God is relegated into the obscure background, because the crisis so completely dominates the foreground. This is not to say that God is not important to either the process or content of caregiving, but it is to say that a person's view of God may be skewed or otherwise distorted by intense anxiety over the crisis.

Yet, even when placed in the obscure background by the careseeker, a person's God may function powerfully by acting as a focal point or even vanishing point. Let me give an illustration from drawing. In order for a picture to correctly represent reality to the viewer, it must be drawn in perspective. This, of course, gives the field of vision appreciable depth. To give perspective, the artist selects what is called a vanishing point. All lines are then oriented toward that point. The vanishing point functions as the farthest place in the background. It appears to be where everything would vanish on the horizon; yet, at the same time it is where all the lines of perspective are oriented. I want to suggest that a person's God may function in an analogous manner. Because a God-representation is a central feature of a person's sense of self, the caregiver does not have to worry about bringing God into the foreground, because all lines lead to the person's God, and thus all associations are oriented in some way in that direction.

The caregiver's task is then to empathically guide the caregiver toward increased self-understanding through insight. The caregiver may have to help the careseeker ferret out the patterns or uncover enough lines of perspective in order to find the direction. The caregiver will have to help the careseeker remain focused and oriented by containing the inevitable anxiety that will obscure or sometimes obliterate the path.

Pastoral theology also functions to orient and inform the caregiver. A person's God can be understood a number of ways, but theologically this God can be viewed as a person's limited and finite way to create an ordered and meaningful world. Because a God-representation is just that, a representation, it is a product of human limitation and finitude. A person's God will never adequately portray the reality of God and perhaps even the reality of the self, in part because a child initially forms it in order to modulate parental failures. That is, the God-representation is formed in order to deal with perceived powerlessness of the parents. It is the person's way to order and control what otherwise would be chaos.

The child forms God-representations in his or her own self-interest. That is, God-representations are formed in the interest of the survival and well-being of the self. I do not mean that humans are flawed by design or are destined to use their God to further selfish gains. I do mean, however, that by design, humans have a capacity and a propensity to reach out for God. Persons have a narcissistic investment in God, but that narcissism may need healing and often does.

God-representations are a way humans incarnate ultimate meanings and values. But because these incarnations reflect the life history and experience of an individual, they develop and change. That is, God-representations must "grow" in order to remain fertile, vital selfobjects. As a person maintains a sense of personal continuity, so, too, would his or her God-representations.

Understanding God-representations as selfobjects implies that salvation occurs in real historical time within the context of real relationships. When John fled further interpersonal intimacy, he cut himself off from an avenue of God's saving grace. John's intense psychic pain led him away from those who could most help him and love him. It led him toward greater self-absorption and greater solitude.

For there to be a change in someone's God-representations, there must first be a change in the person's object relations. This suggests that God acts through incarnate love. This also suggests that God saves through the incarnate grace of the faith community. For John, then, healing began with constant, reassuring empathy from real persons. For many people the need for very reliable constancy, affirmation, and validation experienced through empathy can occur only within the bounds of the caregiver-careseeker relationship. As real relationships proceed in the direction of greater depth and scope, so too may such a person's relationship with God. But if relationships do not lead in that direction, further experience will result in greater bondage and greater psychological distress.

Because church professionals and their families are official institutional incarnations of God's love, they should not be surprised that relationships with people are subject to the same distortions and dynamics as individuals' God-representations. That is, a person will use the church professional in a way related to how he or she uses God-representations.

A member of a congregation may be hostile or solicitous because he or she is equally hostile or solicitous toward God. Most pastors and pastors' spouses know this. My experience as both a pastor's wife and minister of counseling confirms this. So what I am suggesting is far from original, but I am underscoring that if, for example, a person or other staff member is angry with God, and wants counseling, the pastor would be well advised to refer that person for counseling elsewhere, because of the negative transference sure to be experienced in the pastoral relationship. Such a caring relationship would be especially volatile if the careseeker held key leadership roles in the local church.

Finally, a person's experience with a God-representation is not only a religious experience or a psychological experience, but a personal expression of faith. It is an enactment of what it means for that person to be who he or she is at that time, in that place, with particular persons. It is also an enactment of what it means to be with God at a particular time and place. Part of John's problem was that he seemingly could not take a leap of faith. John could not wrestle with God's angel and ask why God had apparently failed him.

Wrestling with angels or demons takes strength and courage. Someone who is wounded and weary from pain may not have the needed strength or courage to be or do. He or she may need to call upon others to help "shore up" his or her vulnerable self and to see him or her through the crisis. In his suffering, John felt totally alone, and he feared that if he wrestled with God, he would die. He also feared that God might leave him. In a sense, John sacrificed himself to save his God.

When John felt the real, personal presence of God in his hospital room, he was too weak to resist. He had already suffered traumatic empathic failure many times in his life. But to understand that hospital experience John needed the shoring up from other real persons. Real relationships seemingly meant only empathic failure, and John fled to what he thought was solace, his evoked companion par excellence. John fled to his God and away from interpersonal intimacy. In so doing, he fled from the possibility of wholeness.

A biblical account found in Genesis gives us a story that contrasts with John's. When Jacob wrestled with the angel, he realized that he was wounded; a vital part of his self was hurt. But Jacob did not let the angel go. Jacob knew he had looked God in the face and lived. Before the angel left, he blessed Jacob and changed his name to Israel. After this fateful encounter with God, Jacob, now Israel, met his archrival, his brother Esau. As Jacob, he had tricked and cheated his brother, tricked him out of his birthright and cheated him out of his father's blessing. After an encounter with God, Israel "drew near" to his brother and reconciled. As Jacob, he wrestled with his God, but then as Israel, he put contention away and reconciled with his brother. The point is that an encounter with his God enabled Jacob to enter into significant intimate relationships, not flee interpersonal intimacy, but he entered into them as a transformed self signified by his new name.

If God-representations are important in maintaining psychic balance and if they emanate from the core of the self, so, too, must faith and faith issues be at the core of the self. Faith is more than cognitive belief; it is part of the total matrix of a person's sense of self. Hence a person's faith and the selfobjects with which he or she portrays that faith are central to understanding that person's interpersonal relationships.

The presence of God is often experienced as immanently real. It is sometimes understood as a sign of divine favor and received as a precious, although heavy, gift. It may be understood as a sign of God's personal and abiding love.

For some, it is only in this relationship that they sense acceptance and affirmation of their fragile sense of self.

Images of God may tell a caregiver what it means to the careseeker to experience empathic response. Because God-representations are forged within a particular sense of self, they reflect the history of the self. But because God-representations may embody a person's expectations of good-enough empathy, they may also provide significant clues as to how to guide a careseeker toward holy ground. They may, in any case, suggest what care means to the careseeker. In order to offer empathy to careseekers, caregivers need a clear understanding of who careseekers' Gods are and how these Gods came to be part of personal histories, so that they may guide, sustain, heal, and reconcile persons toward relationships of greater depth and scope and hence a more productive future.

Annotated Bibliography

Allport, Gordan. *The Individual and His Religion*. New York: Macmillan Co., 1950.
Classic work regarding the relation of religious and personality development. Core concept: God may become the supreme expression of personality.

Basch, Michael F. "Selfobjects, Development, and Psychotherapy." In *Kohut's Legacy*, edited by Paul E. Stepansky and Arnold Goldberg, 157–70. Hillsdale, N.J.: Analytic Press, 1984.
Relation between selfobjects and development as it effects adult psychopathology. Core concept: What the cell is to biology, the selfobject is to psychotherapy.

_____. "Selfobjects and Selfobject Transference: Theoretical Implications." In *Kohut's Legacy: Contributions to Self Psychology*, edited by Paul E. Stepansky and Arnold Goldbery, 21–42. Hillsdale, N.J.: Analytic Press, 1984.
Definition and history of Kohut's constructs of selfobject and selfobject transferences given in a developmental context. Specifically, self psychology's understanding of Oedipal development is distinguished from more traditional psychoanalysis.

Bohler, Carolyn. "Metaphors for God in Pastoral Counseling." *Circuit Rider* 11 (March 1987): 3–4. God-language crucial when working with life-stage issues in counseling.

Bollinger, Richard A. "Difference between Pastoral Counseling and Psychotherapy." *Bulletin of the Menninger Clinic* 49 (1985): 371–86.
Unique aspects of pastoral counseling in terms of context, content, resources. Emphasizes pastor's representative function.

Chessick, Richard D. *Psychology of the Self and the Treatment of Narcissism*. Northvale, N.J.: Jason Aronson, 1985.
Distinguishes Kohut from other object relation theorists, including Melanie Klein and Otto Kernberg. Also distinguishes between concepts of ego and self. Extensive discussion of empathy as the use of the clinician's self to imagine client's inner experience.

Freud, Sigmund. *Inhibitions, Symptoms, and Anxiety*. Vol. 18 of *The Standard Edition of the Complete Psychological Works of Sigmund Freud*, translated from the German under general editorship of James Strachey, in collaboration with Anna Freud, assisted by Alix Strachey and Alan Tyson. London: Hogarth Press, 1961.
Distinguishes inhibitions from symptoms. Freud describes signal anxiety.

_____. *On Narcissism*. Vol. 14 of *The Standard Edition of the Complete Psychological Works of Sigmund Freud*, translated from German under general editorship of James Strachey, in collaboration with Anna Freud, assisted by Alix Strachey and Alan Tyson. London: Hogarth Press, 1961.
Freud's theory of narcissism.

_____. *Two Encyclopedia Articles: (A) Psychoanalysis.* Vol. 18 of *The Standard Edition of the Complete Psychological Works of Sigmund Freud,* translated from the German under general editorship of James Strachey, in collaboration with Anna Freud, assisted by Alix Strachey and Alan Tyson. London: Hogarth Press, 1961.

One of Freud's papers on technique.

Gay, Volney P. *Understanding the Occult.* Minneapolis: Fortress Press, 1989.

Title presents the conundrum of the book's primary question: How can we understand occult phenomena? A multidisciplinary application of psychoanalytic theory.

Gerkin, Charles. *The Living Human Document: Re-Visioning Pastoral Counseling in a Hermeneutical Mode.* Nashville: Abingdon Press, 1984.

Basic question: "How can pastoral counseling be at the same time both an authentically theological and a scientifically psychological discipline?" Core issue is a dialogue between theology and psychology.

Golden, Helen K. "Some Thoughts on Psychoanalytic Change: A Self Psychological View." *Contemporary Psychoanalysis* 24 (Jan. 1988): 61–73.

Addresses curative factors in psychoanalysis. Gives a clear definition of selfobject and selfobject transference.

Greenlee, Lynn F. "Kohut's Self Psychology and Theory of Narcissism: Some Implications Regarding the Fall and Restoration of Humanity." *Journal of Psychology and Theology* 14 (1986): 110–16.

Sketches Kohut's understanding of narcissism and then enters into a theological inquiry that delineates his own anthropology and soteriology.

Hartmann, Heinz. *Ego Psychology and the Proof Adaptation.* Translated by David Rapaport. New York: International Universities Press, 1958.

Thesis: Not every adaptation to the environment, or every learning and maturation process, is conflictual.

Hiltner, Seward. *Pastoral Counseling.* Nashville: Abingdon, 1949.

A classic in the field of pastoral care. Provides an introduction to pastoral counseling by presenting concrete, practical facts and fundamental theory and showing their interrelation. A pastor must know the depths (psychological) and be an expert in the heights (theological).

Jordan, Merle R. *Taking on the Gods: The Task of the Pastoral Counselor.* Nashville: Abingdon Press, 1986.

Sees pastoral counseling as a ministry to interpret psychotherapy from a psycho-spiritual or "operational" theology, by which he means a clinical theology. Hypothesizes the origins of neuroses in idolatry.

Kohut, Heinz. *The Analysis of the Self: A Systematic Approach to the Psychoanalytic Treatment of Narcissistic Personality Disorders.* New York: International Universities Press, 1971.

Asserts that there is an independent line of development of narcissism in the self. One can see the struggle in Kohut as he attempts to formulate an alternative model to a conflict or instinctual drive theory of motivation. One can also begin to see Kohut's shift in paradigm from Freud's "Guilty Man" to his own "Tragic Man."

_____. *How Does Analysis Cure?* Edited by Arnold Goldberg with collaborator Paul E. Stepansky. Chicago: University of Chicago Press, 1984.

If one only reads one book by Kohut, this should be the one. Despite some lack of

conceptual clarity of the term *selfobject*, this is Kohut's clearest statement of his
theoretical position and distinctiveness.

———. "Introspection, Empathy, and Psychoanalysis." In *The Search for the Self:
Selected Writings of Heinz Kohut*, edited and with an introduction by Paul H.
Ornstein, 205–32. New York: International Universities Press, 1978.
Kohut distinguishes between ego psychology and self psychology. He also defines
the limits of empathy, which is described as the methodological tool of therapy.

———. *The Kohut Seminars of Self Psychology and Psychotherapy with Adolescents and
Young Adults*. Edited by Miriam Elson. New York: W. W. Norton & Co., 1987.
Kohut relates values, religion, and the self.

———. "A Note on Female Sexuality." In *The Search for the Self: Selected Writings of
Heinz Kohut*, edited and with an introduction by Paul H. Ornstein, 783–92. New
York: International Universities Press, 1978.
Distinguishes his views on female sexuality as opposed to Freud's.

———. "Psychoanalysis and the Interpretation of Literature: A Correspondence with
Erich Heller." *Critical Inquiry* 4 (1978): 433–50.
Shows that the values and meanings that are continuously created by art, religion,
philosophy, and science are an attempt by humankind to recapture the lost wholeness of the self. In this view, persons are motivated by the loss of the secure cohesion, continuity, and harmony of the self. Humans are motivated to find values and
meanings through deficits rather than solely by conflicts.

———. "Remarks about the Formation of the Self." In *The Search for the Self: Selected
Writings of Heinz Kohut*. Edited and with an introduction by Paul H. Ornstein,
737–70. New York: International Universities Press, 1978.
Revision of theory of self formation.

———. *Restoration of the Self*. New York: International Universities Press, 1977.
Defines a "core" sense of self.

Kohut, Heinz, and Ernest Worf. "The Disorders of the Self and Their Treatment: An
Outline." *International Journal of Psycho-Analysis* 59 (1978): 413–25.
Provides a summary of concepts and theories with clinical (diagnostic and thera-
peutic) formulations.

Lang, Joan A. "Notes toward a 'Psychology of the Feminine Self.'" In *Kohut's Legacy*,
edited by Paul E. Stepansky and Arnold Goldbery, 51–70. Hillsdale, N.J.: Analytic
Press, 1984.
Makes important distinctions between male and female Oedipal development.
Female is not seen as a defective male. For a female the quest for wholeness is not
intrinsically a search for a penis.

Lang, Martin A. *Acquiring Our Image of God: Emotional Basis for Religious Education*.
New York: Paulist Press, 1983.
Although not written from the self psychology point of view, attempts to relate psy-
chological images of God with a person's faith experience.

Langer, Suzanne K. *Philosophy in a New Key*. Cambridge: Harvard University Press,
1957.
Cited not only for its own merits, but because Langer is one of Rizzuto's sources for
her concept "representation." Some of Langer's core claims are: humans use sym-

bols to attain and organize belief, the essential act of thought is symbolization, and our sense data perceptions are primarily symbols.

Lovinger, Robert J. *Working with Religious Issues in Therapy*. New York: Jason Aronson, 1984.

Contains a review and critique of Rizzuto. Concludes that the nature of an image of God is often a useful place to begin to survey the nature of parental object-representations.

McDargh, John. "God, Mother, and Me: An Object Relational Perspective on Religious Material." *Pastoral Psychology* 34 (Summer 1986): 251–63.

Uses clinical material from the work of D. W. Winnicott and a case from pastoral work. Avoids the reductionism of Freud, but, in essence, reduces God to a transitional object.

_____. *Psychoanalytic Object Relations Theory and the Study of Religion: On Faith and the Imaging of God*. Lanham, Md.: University Press of America, 1983.

Examines the significance of contemporary psychoanalytic object relations theory as it relates to faith. Uses case material.

Meissner, W. W. "Psychoanalytic Aspect of Religious Experience." In *Annual of Psychoanalysis*, vol. 6. New York: International University Press, 1982.

Uses work of Kohut, Winnicott, and James Fowler to postulate a developmental sequence of religious experience.

Oates, Wayne E. *The Christian Pastor*. 3d ed. revised. Philadelphia: Westminster Press, 1982.

A classic in the field of pastoral care. This is a basic primer by an author with much pastoral experience of various kinds.

_____. *The Presence of God in Pastoral Counseling*. Waco, Texas: Word Books, 1986.

Core claim: God as the center of counseling moves dialogue to trialogue. One goal of counseling is to find an occasional treasure of "simple wisdom." Includes Oates's discussion of the worship dimension of pastoral counseling.

Oden, Thomas C. *Pastoral Theology: Essentials of Ministry*. San Francisco: Harper & Row, 1982.

An attempt to develop an internally consistent grasp of classical Christian thinking about the pastor and provide a foundation for that knowledge of the pastoral office requisite to the practice of ministry. Sources include the Bible and various patristic and classical writers.

Olsson, Peter A. "The Psychotherapy of a Modern Warlock: Rapprochement in a Coven of White Witches." *American Journal of Psychotherapy* 39 (April 1985): 263–76.

Case study within the scope of object relations theory. Material used to demonstrate the phenomenological fit of various supernatural polarities such as good/bad, white/black, God/Satan, man/woman, saint/sinner, angel/demon with primitive narcissistic-borderline defenses such as denial, projection, splitting, and projective identification. In this case the concept of rapprochement is especially helpful.

Paul, Irving H. "The Concept of Schema in Memory Theory." In *Motives and Thought: Psychoanalytic Essays in Honor of David Rapaport*, edited by Robert Holt, vol. 18/19, 218–58. New York: International Universities Press, 1967.

Core claim: Memory is a reconstruction based *on* the past, not *of* the past. Memory is a function of the present. Memory is dynamic and telescopic. Thus what a patient remembers is influenced heavily by the analyst's interpretation. The question of *what* is remembered is also taken up. Recalled experiences are parts of preexisting schema or patternings of reality. Paul builds upon Freud's observations about memory, using work by others such as Jean Piaget.

Propst, L. Rebecca. *Psychotherapy in a Religious Framework: Spirituality in the Emotional Healing Process.* New York: Human Sciences Press, 1988.

Uses cognitive theory to discuss healing process. Particularly in chapter 7, Propst discusses image transformation. For Propst, images are major therapeutic tools because they are immediate, direct, and less likely to be interpreted in terms of preconceived ideas. In particular, images of Jesus can play a central role in correcting self-definitions.

Rizzuto, Ana-Maria. *The Birth of the Living God: A Psychoanalytic Study.* Chicago: University of Chicago Press, 1979.

A clinical study of the possible origins of the individual's private representation of God and its subsequent elaboration. Both belief and unbelief are examined. Argues quite well for a clinical methodology; yet, she does not go to the same extent to justify her use of particular theoretical frames. Her core claim is that for a psychoanalyst to understand a client at all, the client's God needs to be personalized and specific. Rizzuto's theoretical contribution is that, contrary to Freud, a person's God may have pre-Oedipal origins.

_____. "The Father and the Child's Representation of God: A Developmental Approach." In *Father and Child,* edited by Stanley H. Cath, Alan R. Gurwitt, and John Munder Ross, Boston: Little, Brown and Co., 1982.

Central question: What do children do with the parental representations that they transform into God? Argues that representations of God may be understood developmentally.

_____. "Freud, God, and Devil and the Theory of Object Representation." *International Review of Psychoanalysis* 3 (1976): 165–80.

Rizzuto lays out her understanding of Freudian theory in regard to how a person acquires a representation of God and the devil. Argues that Freud's theory does not account for reasons that representations of God and the devil become sources of belief.

_____. "Object Relations and the Formation of the Image of God." *British Journal of Medical Psychology* 47 (1974): 83–94.

Presents two clinical cases that illustrate the formation of an individual's God-image out of early object relations, that is, prior to Oedipal stage.

Rossi, Albert S. "Change in the Client and in the Client's God." In *Psychotherapy and the Religiously Committed Patient,* edited by E. Mark Stern. New York: Haworth Press, 1985.

Often the client's image of God acts as a barometer of the psychological change experienced in therapy.

Rowe, Crayton E. Jr., and David S. MacIsaac. *Empathic Attunement: The "Technique" of Psychoanalytic Self Psychology.* Northvale, N.J.: Jason Aronson, 1989.

Simple and easy-to-understand exposition of Kohut, including his notions of empathy, selfobject, various defenses including horizontal and vertical splitting, and selfobject transferences.

Socarides, Daphne D., and Robert D. Stolorow. "Affects and Selfobjects." In *The Annual of Psychoanalysis*, vol. 12/13, 105–19. New York: International Universities Press, 1985. Deals with the relation of affect to the developing sense of self. Core claim: Selfobject functions pertain fundamentally to the affective dimension of self-experience, and the need for selfobjects pertains to the need for specific, requisite responsiveness to varying affect states throughout development. This article expands and refines the concept of selfobject in that selfobjects are instrumental in the integration of affect throughout the life cycle. Further, authors suggest that objects may split into good and bad affects. This article also helps us understand the importance of empathy within the context of therapy, particularly in regard to the therapist as a selfobject that may modulate, grade, and contain the client's strong affect.

Spero, Moshe H. "Identity and Individuality in the Nouveau-Religious Patient: Theoretical and Clinical Aspects." *Psychiatry* 50 (Feb. 1987): 55–64. Shows the continuing interest in the psychotherapy community in extending the significance of the psychological function of religious beliefs from merely the infantile wish-fulfillment aspects of religiosity toward the broader domain of ego functioning and quality of object relations. Core claim: There is need to understand and distinguish between the development of religious belief in persons whose ideological commitment is relatively constant from earliest childhood and its development in those who adopt or modify religious belief in later life, in conjunction with the implications for therapy. Spero says that clinical experience shows the change in religious perspective represents a "significant psychosocial crisis, requiring certain important prepsychological tasks in order in achieve successful resolution." The goal of therapy with such persons involves not only healing the conflict but nurturing the movement through the successive developmental phases, helping the person integrate past and present self- and object-representations, thus fostering a new sense of past with which the person can identify.

———. "The Reality and the Image of God in Psychotherapy." *American Journal of Psychotherapy* 39 (Jan. 1985): 75–85. A carefully and helpfully articulated look at the issues surrounding belief in God and the reality of God as they relate to the patient/therapist relationship. Spero says that while the psychotherapist cannot arbitrate moral claims and decisions for patients, nor claim to possess the single true understanding of religious experience, the therapist can invite the patient to examine the moral implications of his or her psychological experiences and the psychological impact and consequences of his or her religious experiences.

Stern, Daniel N. "Affect in the Context of the Infant's Lived Experience: Some Considerations." *International Journal of Psycho-Analysis* 69 (1988): 223–28. Addresses and raises some issues about affective experience, the memories of affective experience, and how such memories become representations.

———. *The Interpersonal World of the Infant*. New York: Basic Books, 1985. Central questions: How do babies experience the world around them? Stern postulates four senses of self: an emergent self, a core self, a subjective self, and a verbal self. Core claims: Sense of self is always experienced as separate from sense of other from (at least) birth. Baby never experiences "blooming, buzzing, confusion," that is, the interpersonal world of the infant is experienced as ordered from the beginning. This book is a synthesis of psychoanalysis and developmental psychology.

Sullivan, Harry S. *Conceptions of Modern Psychiatry*. New York: W. W. Norton & Co., 1940. In this book, Sullivan sets forth his central ideas of an interpersonal theory of personality, including his theory of anxiety, the self-system, dynamics of change, and motivation.

———. *The Interpersonal Theory of Psychiatry*. Edited by Helen Perry and Mary Gawel. New York: W. W. Norton & Co., 1953. A classic in the field of psychotherapy because it led psychiatry toward a keener recognition of social factors involved in mental health and disorder. Sullivan defines the method of psychiatry as participant observation and puts forth his developmental schema, which he divides into: infancy, childhood, the juvenile era, preadolescence, adolescence, late adolescence, and adulthood. Each phase of development has its own needs and conflicts that must be resolved.

———. *The Psychiatric Interview*. New York: W. W. Norton & Co., 1954. A formulation of the technique of psychotherapy which proceeds step-by-step from reconnaissance to detailed inquiry. Included is Sullivan's theory of communication, which includes his conceptualization of transference, or as he calls it, "parataxic distortion." If reading only one of Sullivan's books, this is the one to read, because it explicates all of Sullivan's major concepts and contributions.

Taylor, Graeme. "Demoniacal Possession and Psychoanalytic Theory." *British Journal of Medical Psychology* 51 (1978): 53–60. Discusses the psychoanalytic treatment of a case of demoniacal possession to indicate the multiple dynamic meanings that possession may have and to demonstrate the necessity for integrating and applying aspects of libido and object relations theories. Claims that such a study contributes much to the understanding of particularly borderline and psychotic states. Includes a literature review.

Ulanov, Ann B. *Picturing God*. Cambridge: Cowley, 1986. This book is largely a reprint of Ulanov's earlier articles from 1984 to 1985. From a Jungian perspective, Ulanov posits that one goal of therapy, and particularly pastoral counseling, is to reach through the person's God-images to the God who breaks images. Contrary to Freud, Ulanov says the whole person never can (nor should ?) completely leave behind the infantile.

White, Marjorie, Weiner Taggart, and Marcella Bakur. *The Theory and Practice of Self Psychology*. New York: Brunner/Mazel, 1986. An overview of the basic concepts of self psychology, including selfobject, maturity, fragmentation of the self, empathy, transmuting internalization, and self psychology's developmental scheme. The authors also discuss aggression, positing that aggression is a reaction to a provocation rather than an inevitable discharge. Also takes up the argument that drive theory is not sufficient to account for the human sense of a supraordinate self.

Winnicott, D. W. *Holding and Interpretation: Fragment of an Analysis*. Introduction and edited by M. Masud R. Khan. New York: Grove Press, 1986. A clinical illustration of analysis as a holding environment as offered by Winnicott. Offers an opportunity to view Winnicott, the therapist, at work.